Our 24 Family Ways
Family Devotional Guide

An *Our Family* Devotional Tool for training your children in biblical values and Christian character.

by Clay Clarkson

Whole Heart Press
Books to build hearts for God

Our 24 Family Ways: Family Devotional Guide
Copyright © 1998, 2004 by Clay Clarkson

Design and layout by Rob Lamb
Illustrations by Marvin Jarboe
Cover by Alpha Advertising
Printed in the United States of America

ISBN 1-888692-07-3

Published by:
Whole Heart Ministries
www.wholeheart.org

Whole Heart Ministries is a non-profit ministry dedicated to
helping Christian parents raise wholehearted Christian children.

Table of Contents

Dedication

Train up a child in the way he should go,
even when he is old he will not depart from it.
Proverbs 22:6

I have no greater joy than this,
to hear of my children walking in the truth.
1 John 1:4

This revised edition of **Our 24 Family Ways** is dedicated to my four wholehearted children who walk the path of life with me—Sarah, Joel, Nathan and Joy. This book will be forgotten all too quickly, but your faith is a legacy to future generations, and into eternity.

It is also dedicated to the many families who will use the Ways to set their children's feet on the path of life. It is both humbling and gratifying that you would allow me to join you on your journey of Christian parenting. Thank you!

Special Thanks

To my family, for living out the Ways for all these years.
To Sally, for unfailing encouragement as a companion on the path of life.
To Sarah, for helping to write the Story Starters for all 24 Ways.
To Marvin Jarboe, a gracious Christian and very talented illustrator, for bringing the Ways to life in his wonderful drawings, and adding his creative touches throughout.

Our 24 Family Ways

Our 24 Family Ways was born out of the simple realization that Christian character is shaped as much by the language we use as it is by the lifestyle we choose. Think about it for a moment. How are family values really transmitted from one generation to the next? The hand-off will occur when your children say to their children, "In our family, we..." and a value for work or self-control or devotion is passed along. We can hold a value dearly only when it is expressed clearly in language.

Our 24 Family Ways is simply our attempt to create the language of values for our family. As our children learn to speak that language, and live it, then they will be able to pass it on to their children. We are sharing it with you in the hope that it will be of eternal value to your family as well. Of course, the words of God's Word are the most important language you can pass on to your children. That's why each of the 24 family Ways is reinforced by five defining Scripture verses or passages. Each Way is a practical principle for Christian living, drawn from the deep well of biblical truth and wisdom, and expressed in language that is easy for you and your children to understand and remember. It is God's truth for family life.

If you are like most of the Christian parents we know, you want to teach your children the Bible, instill biblical values deep in their hearts, train them in Christian character and godly living, and strengthen their relationship with the Lord. That's what we wanted for our children, which gave birth to **Our 24 Family Ways**. This simple resource, created by real parents for real children, is designed to help you accomplish each of those goals in your own children's lives. In addition to the 24 Ways, or values, in six key areas of Christian family life, it is filled with 120 carefully selected related scriptures, 24 character quality definitions, and 120 complete family devotional outlines. It is a resource to help you disciple your children.

Our 24 Family Ways is a tool, though, not a detailed "how to" plan or an unbending list of "rules." It is a tool you can use to help you build your children's character, and like most tools it has both strengths and limitations. So keep a few thoughts in mind as you use it:

• **Our 24 Family Ways** is a flexible resource, not a rigid regimen that must be religiously followed. Set your own pace, pick and choose what you want to use, change the order, add scriptures that you like personally or think might work better, create your own ARTS questions. Fit it to your own family's needs and experience.

• We used primarily instructional and wisdom verses rather than longer historical narratives, which require more time to read and more explanation of the historical context. We encourage you, though, to select a related Bible story that can be read for a weekend family night when there is more time for discussion, role play, and other activities. Children respond naturally to stories, and Bible stories are rich in character issues. Check our website for suggested Bible stories.

• The Bible verses used for the devotions generally were chosen because we felt they would work best for family discussion. Keep in mind that they do not constitute a "doctrine" of the related Way or character quality, but rather a thoughtful selection of representative scriptures that reinforce that Way. These are broad biblical principles, not legalistic biblical standards. Always use them with grace.

• For Scripture memory verses, we include the New International Version (NIV), the New American Standard Bible version (NASB), and the New King James Version (NKJV), one of which should suit the tastes and preferences of your family. However, because it is generally clearer and more easily understood by younger children, questions in the ARTS outlines are based on the NIV text. We use the "classic" NIV text.

Family Bible Times

It is hard for any family in this time-challenged, fast-paced culture in which we live to carve out a place in the daily schedule for regular family devotions. We, too, have struggled at times with keeping our family devotions a daily priority. Two factors have helped us stay faithful.

First, we have a time. For our family it has been breakfast, when we're all fresh from a good night's sleep (usually) and ready to start a new day. Second, we have a plan. It may be a resource such as this one, or a trusted devotional book, or reading through the Bible one chapter a day, or studying a new biblical topic each week. Whatever we do, though, we try to avoid the careless "flip-and-dip devotional" syndrome that so easily becomes a default plan.

But faithfulness alone-to have a time and to have a plan-will not necessarily ensure that you always have a "successful" family devotion. How you do what you do with the time and the plan will determine your success. We've always found it helpful to maintain a distinction between Bible study time and family devotional time. In Bible study, I want to help my children understand the Word of God; in family devotions, I want to help my children relate to the God of the Word. Both are important for their growth, but many good parents who fail to make the distinction carelessly allow family devotional time to become Bible study time, and inadvertently impoverish their family's spiritual growth in the process.

It has always been our conviction that the primary goal of a family devotional should be not only to "learn the Bible," but to "love the Bible." Children can learn the Bible and not love it, but they cannot love the Bible and not learn it! Our goal is to create a spiritually-enriching atmosphere in which we all genuinely love to open the Word and listen to God, to talk and think and laugh and pray because something in his wonderful Word touches our spirits. We have great confidence that if our children grow up loving God's Word, then the learning of God's Word will take care of itself.

Of course, if our children never see their parents reading the Bible, or never hear us say how a verse has ministered to us, or share with them how God's Spirit spoke to us in our devotions, then we shouldn't be surprised if they don't make the step from participating in a family devotional time to developing a personal devotional time. **Our 24 Family Ways** can help create a lively family devotional time, provide some good scriptures to discuss, and it can stimulate some good family prayer, all of which help model a devotional habit. But there is one thing it can never do–it cannot replace the personal example of a godly parent.

Family Devotional ARTS Outlines

At the heart of **Our 24 Family Ways** is an outline we use for Bible discussion we call our Family Devotional ARTS. You can use this uncomplicated, easy-to-remember, and easy-to-use outline for any of your own family Bible reading times or family devotions. All you do is pick a good Bible passage and then apply the ARTS outline to it. We've done it for you in the 120 devotions in this book, but here's how you can do it with any Bible passage.

A = Ask a question

The first thing you want to do in a family devotional time is gain the interest and attention of your children. Without interest there is no openness; without attention there is no responsiveness. Take some time to consider the verse or passage you want to discuss, and frame an open-ended question that will generate conversation and interaction–one that will elicit an opinion or insight, rather than just an answer. Personalize the question. Try to be creative so that the question will lead you naturally into the Scripture reading. For example, if you were to read the story of David and Goliath, ask your children what it might be like to be nine feet tall.

R = Read the Bible

Once you have your children interested and interacting, turn to your Scripture text and read it aloud. It is at this point that you will either heighten their interest, or deflate it, depending on how you read. You can show that it really is God's "living and active" Word, or you can turn it into a "dead and dull" spiritual textbook reading. Don't lose their interest with a dry-as-toast reading of God's Word. Learn how to read the Bible aloud with dramatic expression, timing, and emphasis. Be aware of your pacing–don't read too quickly, or too slowly. Show them with your voice that you believe the Bible is alive with truth.

T = Talk about it

After reading the passage, begin to ask some probing questions about the content. Your goal is not just to elicit content recognition ("What did David say to Goliath?"), but also to help your children find examples, principles, and life applications within the passage ("How did David express his faith in God?" or "What are other kinds of giants we have to face?"). You are leading them through a mini-inductive study of the passage, showing them how to observe (What does it say?), interpret (What does it mean?), and apply (What does it mean to me?). Help your children see more than just words on a page. Help them to learn how to hear God's voice in His Word, and how to apply it to their every-day lives.

S = Speak to God

Personal application of the Scripture is important, but too often an artificial "do this today" tacked on at the end of a devotion can rob that Bible time of what should be the real application–prayer. You want to help your children understand that the first and most natural response, or application, to reading the Word should always be to speak to God about it. It is important for you to teach your children how to pray by suggesting specific words and ways, or even how to pray the Scripture passage itself. You are showing how to make the application a personal response to God rather than just an impersonal conclusion to the devotional. But once you tell them, then be sure to pray!

Instructions

- Use your own Bible! We purposely designed **Our 24 Family Ways** to need a Bible. We want it to be a devotional tool that affirms the centrality of the Bible in your family, not displaces it. In the end, your Bible is the real devotional product, not this book, which is really just a tool for opening God's word.

- **Our 24 Family Ways** is designed to be used best at meal times or similar gatherings when everyone in the family is together, sitting down, and relaxed. You can use just your Bible and this copy of the book, or you can add other products in the O24FW family to help, such as the **Kids Color-In Book**, laminated poster, or a Flip-a-Way Chart.

- Read over the ARTS outline each day before using it. You can use one or both of the questions (Ask), or make up your own. Familiarize yourself with the Scripture passage (Read) and the questions for it (Talk). If you would like to add more insight about the passage, review a commentary or study Bible prior to the devotion time. Read aloud the prayer suggestions (Speak) and talk about the application of the Scripture to your lives.

- On the first day of each week, turn to a new Way. Read it, then have everyone repeat it aloud after you. Discuss the illustration ("Story Starter" ideas are provided on the "Learning the Way" page). Read and discuss the character definition, and identify an example of it in your own family. Read and recite the Scripture memory verse or passage. You may also review previously learned Ways on the first day using this book or other O24FW products. If you will be using the ARTS outlines for your family devotions, do the first one, which always uses the memory verse for that Way.

- Each Way includes five days of devotional outlines. However, you may use as few or as many of the devotionals as you desire for your family. If you use a different devotional resource, you may want to do just the 24 Ways without the ARTS outlines. Or, you may want to use just the "Day 1" outlines. You can set whatever pace is most comfortable for your family—one a week, one a day, or one every now and then.

- Use the "Learning the Way" page included with each Way. That's where you will find commentary about the Way, a character quality and definition, Scripture memory verse texts in three versions, and a "Story Starter" idea to talk about the illustration for that Way. There is also a box for you to make notes, describe a special insight about the Way from one of your children, or record a related family slogan.

- When you complete the book and know all the Ways, read the "We're On the Way" Family Covenant page. Have each family member sign it. Make it a big celebration. Plan a special event. Award prizes. Your all on the Way! Whatever you do to emphasize that learning all the Ways is a really important accomplishment for your family will go a long way to making your children want to remember and use the Ways. Be very positive about them, and they will be positive about them. Be sure they understand the Family Commitment is not just for them, but for the whole family.

Suggestions

- Before you start on Way #1, be sure to review all 24 Ways together as a family. You can use the list provided, or one of the other **O24FW** products. On the "Learning the Way" pages, brief commentary is provided to help you talk about each Way, so you can be sure your children understand what all the words mean, and what the Way means.

- Use the **O24FW Kids Color-In Book** with younger children. They will love coloring in the special line art versions of the illustrations in this book. Or, make a photocopy of the illustration page in this book for each child whenever you begin a new Way (you have permission of make copies for your personal use at home). They can then color the pages and save them in a notebook, or display them on a wall. You can add affirming comments on the backs of the pages when they show they understand that Way.

- Once you have learned all 24 Ways as a family, be sure to review them periodically. A fill-in-the-blanks review page is included, and is also in the **Kids Color-In Book**. Or, purchase and use the laminated wall poster, or the Flip-a-Way Chart. Other helps are available at Whole Heart Online. Also, a page is included after the Ways with all the character quality definitions listed. These can be reviewed, too.

- Scripture memory review card templates for each version used—NIV, NASB and NKJV—are available for free download online at www.wholeheart.org (PDFs require Adobe Reader). Photocopy each sheet onto card stock and cut out the cards along the dotted lines. Make a set for each child.

- "Our Own Way" pages are provided at the back to record new ways, slogans and proverbs unique to your family, and worth preserving! Use these pages, too, to capture those otherwise fleeting wise sayings by you or your children, "inspired" insights about life, or scripture verses that God uses in your family life.

- "Make Your Own Way" template pages are also available for free download online. With them you can make additional Ways to reflect your family's own values. Or, just add your own family slogans to any of the Ways. For example, for Way 13 we often include the slogan, "It's not done at all until it's all done." Slogans are an important and powerful part of your character training and family values language.

- Use the Ways in the context of a normal day. Use them for affirming and suggesting good behavior as much, or even more, as you do for correcting improper behavior. Make a game out of reciting a Way by calling out just its number and having the child recite the Way. You can use them pre-emptively as well. For instance, if your children are going somewhere new, review the Ways group for Behavior; or, if chores need to be done, review the Ways group for Work. Have a Family Ways Day when everybody tries to "do" as many of the Ways as possible (make a Ways checklist wit spaces for notes one each one). Be creative in how you use them in your family life.

Our 24 Family Ways:

Concerning AUTHORITIES in our family...

1   We love and obey our Lord, Jesus Christ, with wholehearted devotion.

2   We read the Bible and pray to God every day with an open heart.

3   We honor and obey our parents in the Lord with a respectful attitude.

4   We listen to correction and accept discipline with a submissive spirit.

Concerning RELATIONSHIPS in our family...

5   We love one another, treating others with kindness, gentleness and respect..

6   We serve one another, humbly thinking of the needs of others first.

7   We encourage one another, using only words that build up and bless others.

8   We forgive one another, covering an offense with love when wronged or hurt.

Concerning POSSESSIONS in our family...

9   We are thankful to God for what we have, whether it is a little or a lot.

10   We are content with what we have, not coveting what others have.

11   We are generous with what we have, sharing freely with others.

12   We take care of what we have, using it wisely and responsibly.

Concerning WORK in our family...

13 We are diligent to complete a task promptly and thoroughly when asked.

14 We take initiative to do all of our own work without needing to be told.

15 We work with a cooperative spirit, freely giving and receiving help.

16 We take personal responsibility to keep our home neat and clean at all times.

Concerning ATTITUDES in our family...

17 We choose to be joyful, even when we feel like complaining.

18 We choose to be peacemakers, even when we feel like arguing.

19 We choose to be patient, even when we feel like getting our own way.

20 We choose to be gracious, even when we don't feel like it.

Concerning CHOICES in our family...

21 We do what we know is right, regardless what others do or say.

22 We ask before we act when we do not know what is right to do.

23 We exercise self-control at all times and in *every* kind of situation.

24 We always tell the truth and do not practice deceitfulness of any kind.

*Train a child in the way he should go,
and when he is old he will not turn from it.*

—Proverbs 22:6

Our Family Way 1

Concerning AUTHORITIES in our family

We love and obey our Lord, Jesus Christ, with wholehearted devotion.

Our Family Way 1

Concerning AUTHORITIES in our family

A → *Ask A Question*

R *Read The Bible*

Day 1

As king, would you share your throne with another king? Why, or why not?

If someone could observe your life for a day, how would they know what is really important to you? What would they see?

Matthew 22:34-40

The religious leaders in Jerusalem wanted to trick Jesus into saying something wrong so they could accuse him of teaching against them. But Jesus knew what to say.

Day 2

Which is easier for you to do: to love your parents, or to obey them? Why?

If you had a "pocket parent" card that played a short digital message every 30 minutes, what would you want to hear? Not hear?

John 14:15-21

Jesus has told his disciples that he is going where they cannot follow. They are confused so he comforts and encourages them, and tells them what to expect when he is gone.

Day 3

What one gift would you want to give to Jesus right now if he were here?

If you were a poor, peasant child and the king made you a prince or princess, would you be a different person, or act differently? Why?

Romans 12:1-2

Because of all that God has done for us in Jesus, Paul teaches that we should stop being worldly, but instead let him change our hearts and minds so we will want to do his will.

Day 4

If you were chosen to select the next president, what qualities or qualifications would you look for in that person?

If your son is to become king after you, what advice would you want to give to him?

1 Chronicles 28:8-10

David has called together all the leaders of Israel to pass the torch of leadership to his son Solomon. He admonishes him to seek and serve the Lord wholeheartedly.

Day 5

You're lost, it's getting dark, but you have directions to get home. Would you take a shortcut home? Why, or why not?

Do you like to follow directions, or do things your own way? Which is better?

Deuteronomy 5:28-33

As Israel prepares to enter the Promised Land, Moses recalls what God said at Mt. Sinai 40 years before, and admonishes the people to fear God, and serve and obey him.

We love and obey our Lord, Jesus Christ, with wholehearted devotion.

Talk About It

Speak To God

What did Jesus mean when he described how a person should love God?

Why does Jesus call it the "first and greatest" commandment?

How can you love God like that today? Think of one way you can do that in your home.

Pray that God will help you love him better today, with everything that is inside of you.

Ask Him to show you any thought or sin in your life that might keep you from loving Him the way He wants you to love Him.

What is the relationship between loving Christ and obeying him?

Why is the Holy Spirit so important? How can he help them love and obey?

What are the "commands" of Jesus?

Tell the Lord that you want to love and obey him today, with your whole heart.

Thank God for the Holy Spirit who lives in your heart and guides you.

Praise God for his love for you.

What is the difference between a "living" sacrifice and a dead sacrifice?

What are some ways you sometimes "conform" to the world's ways of life?

What can you do to "renew" your mind?

Offer your life to God so you can do his "good, pleasing and perfect will" today.

Confess any ways you have been conforming to "the pattern of this world."

Ask God to renew your mind for him so you can do his will.

What specific fatherly and leadership advice did David give to his son, Solomon?

What can you do to follow the same advice in your own life? How can you "seek him"?

What is "wholehearted devotion"?

Praise and "acknowledge" God for his love, goodness and faithfulness to your family.

Ask him to give you a heart and mind to serve him and seek to know him.

Devote your heart fully to him today.

What does it mean to "fear God"?

How would fearing and obeying God give the Israelites and their children a better life?

If God's "way" is a straight and narrow path, what is to the left and right of it?

Thank the Lord that he has made very clear in his word how to live a godly life.

Thank him for the blessings of a happy family that come from trust and obedience.

Pray for a heart that fears and obeys God.

Learning the Way

Our Family Way 1 ~ Concerning AUTHORITIES in our family

We love and obey our Lord, Jesus Christ, with wholehearted devotion.

Commentary

Jesus said that obedience is one of the most important ways that we show our love for him. When we desire to know his will, and then we willingly do what he asks, we show that we really do love him, and that he is Lord in our hearts.

Character: Godliness

Wanting more than anything else to please God in everything that I think, say and do.

Scripture Memory: Matthew 22:37-38

Jesus replied: "Love the Lord your God with all your heart and with all your soul and with all your mind." This is the first and greatest commandment. (NIV)

And He said to him, "'You shall love the Lord your God with all your heart, and with all your soul, and with all your mind.' This is the great and foremost commandment." (NSAB)

Jesus said to him, "You shall love the Lord your God with all your heart, with all your soul, and with all your mind." This is the first and great commandment. (NKJV)

Story Starter

It was a bright, sunny Saturday morning. Dad called out, "Good morning, everyone! Let's all get together in the den for a family devotion to start our day." Just then, the phone rang and Mother went to the other room to answer the call. Then, Nathan's best friend from down the street knocked at the door. He had his baseball bat and glove with him. Jennifer became distracted by a new toy in her room. Even Dad started thinking about playing golf later. What do you suppose Dad did to get everyone together for that time in the Bible?

Notes _____

_____

_____

_____

_____

_____

_____

_____

Our Family Way 2

Concerning AUTHORITIES in our family

We read the Bible and pray to God every day with an open heart.

Our Family Way 2

Concerning AUTHORITIES in our family

A → Ask A Question

R Read The Bible

Day 1

If you were moving away and knew you might never see your best friend again, what would you say to that friend?

As a soldier, what special training do you need before going into a battle?

2 Timothy 3:14-17

The Apostle Paul, knowing he will die soon, gives advice to his beloved follower Timothy about being a Christian leader. He reminds him of the importance of the scriptures.

Day 2

If you and your friends wanted to build a clubhouse, describe how you would do it. Where would you build it? How? Why?

Think of all the different ways that weather and other natural forces can destroy a home.

Matthew 7:24-27

Jesus concludes his "Sermon on the Mount" by reminding his followers that there is only one sure foundation upon which to build your life—the word of God. Any other is foolish.

Day 3

If you were Johnny Appleseed, where would you spread your seeds to make sure they would take root and grow into apple trees?

What does a seed need to grow? What would keep it from growing?

Luke 8:4-15

Jesus describes how different people respond to the word of God. "Good soil" is prepared and ready, so the seed falls in a "noble and good heart" that hears the word and obeys it.

Day 4

What would life be like if you had no mirrors, no reflections, and no way to see yourself?

Create a new Christmas cookie (ex.: fudge-mallow-mel-nut cookies). Would you want to write down the recipe? Why?

James 1:22-25

James, the brother of Jesus, instructs Christians about the nature of the Christian life. He offers pastorly advice and wisdom about "doing" the word, not just "hearing" it.

Day 5

If you were given a treasure map, where would you hide it to keep it safe?

Think of eight words beginning with the letter "B" that describe God's word and what it does in our lives. Now, try "C" and "W."

Psalm 119:9-16

One of 22 passages in Psalm 119, each 8 verses long, using the Hebrew alphabet as a learning method to help students remember the incomparable value of God's word.

We read the Bible and pray to God every day with an open heart.

Talk About It

Speak To God

Talk About It	Speak To God
What Scripture truths have you learned "from infancy" that you can "continue" in? How can the Scripture "teach" us? "rebuke" us? "correct" us? "train" us in righteousness? What do you need to be "equipped" to do?	Thank God for his word that shows you how to live for him every day. Ask God to help you be consistent to read the Bible every day to grow in wisdom. Pray that you will be useful to God.
How do people foolishly build their lives on "sand"? What happens to them? How can you build your life upon "the rock"? What kinds of real-life spiritual storms come against your "house"? Why is "rock" safer?	Thank God for his word that gives you a sure foundation for life. Ask God to help you trust him more every day so you can stand firm in the storms of life. Pray that you will be a wise life-builder.
What would the different people Jesus describes be like if you met them today? Is your life "good soil" that is ready for the seed of God's word? Why, or why not? What makes a heart "noble and good"?	Tell God that your heart is open to him. Pray that his word will stay in your heart, take root, and produce fruit for Christ. Thank him for parents who train your heart, who prepare it to receive God's word.
Why is the word of God like a "mirror"? What does it reflect? What do you see in it? Why is the one who looks "intently" into the word of God called "blessed"? How can you be a "doer" of the word?	Pray that God will help you see yourself in his word every day, and see himself in you. Ask God to show you new ways each day to become a doer of his word. Thank God for his mercies and blessings.
What does it mean to hide the word in your heart? How will that keep you from sinning? What, exactly, is "hidden" in your heart? How can you "delight" in God's commands, and be sure to not "neglect" his word?	Thank God for his word that keeps you from sin and shows you his wisdom and will. Confess any known sins in your heart. Ask God to help you delight, every day, in his word of truth, and seek it with all your heart.

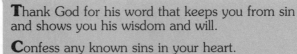

Learning the Way

Our Family Way 2 ~ Concerning AUTHORITIES in our family

We read the Bible and pray to God every day with an open heart.

Commentary

God speaks to us in the Bible, his Word, which is why we need to read it every day. But God wants a relationship, so we also speak to him in prayer. Keeping an "open heart" means we listen carefully for his voice and respond honestly in prayer.

Character: Trust in God

Remembering every day that God loves me and will take care of me.

Scripture Memory: 2 Timothy 3:16-17

All Scripture is God-breathed and is useful for teaching, rebuking, correcting and training in righteousness, so that the man of God may be thoroughly equipped for every good work. (NIV)

All Scripture is inspired by God and profitable for teaching, for reproof, for correction, for training in righteousness; so that the man of God may be adequate, equipped for every good work. (NASB)

All Scripture is given by inspiration of God, and is profitable for doctrine, for reproof, for correction, for instruction in righteousness, that the man of God may be complete, thoroughly equipped for every good work. (NKJV)

Story Starter

Joe loved reading his Bible outside, especially on such a pleasant spring day. He had decided to try reading his Bible in different places every day for his special time with Jesus. Annie, his five-year old little sister saw him reading on the hillside and came out to sit beside him. "Will you read to me, too?" she asked. He smiled and began to read Bible stroies to Annie because he remembered how his mom had read out loud to him when he was little. Why is it important to spend time with God every day?

Notes

Our Family Way 3

Concerning AUTHORITIES in our family

We honor and obey our parents in the Lord with a respectful attitude.

Our Family Way 3

Concerning AUTHORITIES in our family

A → **Ask A Question**

R **Read The Bible**

Day 1

Imagine that you are being honored for being a hero. What things might others do to honor you? How would you feel?

Identify as many real, specific ways as you can that you obey your parents each day.

Ephesians 6:1-3

Paul instructs Christians in a household about their relationships to different authorities. He quotes the fifth commandment (Exodus 20:12) to remind children of their responsibility.

Day 2

If you were a daddy, what wise advice would you give your son about growing up?

What good or godly traits can you see in your grandfather, that are also in your father, and that will be in you also?

Proverbs 4:1-13

In chapters 1-9 of Proverbs, Solomon instructs and admonishes his sons about the value of wisdom, discipline, and understanding. He shows them God's path, his "way of wisdom."

Day 3

What would it be like to live in a city with no policemen? Or, with no parents?

When you become a parent, how will you teach your children to submit to you? What will you do if they rebel or disobey?

Romans 13:1-5

As one of several closing comments, Paul admonishes the Roman believers to "submit" to the governing authorities, who in their case was the rule of Rome. It is God's design.

Day 4

If you are told to "clean up your room today," what are the different ways you could respond or "obey"? Which is right?

Make up a song about obedience to the tune of "Jesus Loves Me" (I'll obey you, yes I will...).

Matthew 21:28-32

After being confronted and challenged by the Jewish religious leaders for his teaching, Jesus tells a parable that suggests that they are not really submitting to God's authority.

Day 5

Give each person in your home a "title" that describes their role (ex.: Mom, High and Exalted Maker of Home and Bread).

What would your family be like if everyone was equal in authority? Describe a day.

Colossians 3:18-4:1

Paul exhorts each person in a household — wives, husbands, children, fathers, servants, masters—to be in submission to whatever authority God has placed over them.

We honor and obey our parents in the Lord with a respectful attitude.

T Talk About It

S Speak To God

Talk About It	Speak To God
How do you obey your parents "in the Lord"? **W**hat is "right" about that? **W**hat does it mean to "honor your father and mother"? How is it different than obeying them? How can you can honor them today?	**T**hank God for your father and mother. **C**onfess to God any ways that you have dishonored or disobeyed them. **P**ray that God will help you to honor and obey them better every day.
What did Solomon learn from his father, David? Listen for the action words. **W**hy is wisdom so important? **I**f you "forget...or swerve" from your parents' teaching, what will happen? Why?	**T**hank God for the wisdom that you receive from your parents. **P**ray that God will keep you from forgetting or swerving from their teaching. **P**ray for a heart that receives wisdom.
Which "authorities" do you submit to regularly in your life? Why? What is their role? **H**ow could you rebel against them? Do you? **W**hat does your conscience tell you about submitting to those in authority over you?	**T**hank God for all the legitimate authorities that he has placed over your life. **C**onfess to God any ways that you may have wrongly rebelled against them. **P**ray for a clean conscience.
Describe each son's response to his father. **W**ho does Jesus say enters the kingdom of God? Why do they, and why others not? **I**f someone rebels against authority and sins, what should they do? (32)	**P**ray that God will train your heart to obey your parents quickly and completely. **R**epent of (stop) any sinful habit of arguing with or questioning your parents. **T**ell God you believe in and trust him.
Describe God's "chain of authority" in the Christian home. Where are you? **W**hen Paul says children are to obey their parents in "everything," what does he mean? **W**hy does submission please God?	**T**hank God for parents who fear and honor God, and who submit to his authority. **P**ray that you will have an obedient heart that pleases your parents and God. **P**raise God that he is in authority over you.

Learning the Way

Our Family Way 3 ~ Concerning AUTHORITIES in our family

We honor and obey our parents in the Lord with a respectful attitude.

Commentary

To "honor" parents means to esteem and value them highly. God considers it so important he made it the fifth commandment. Obedience is the best way to honor parents. It is both an external action and an internal attitude if it is truly "in the Lord."

Character: Reverence

Honoring God, my parents and all proper authorities because of who they are in God's eyes.

Scripture Memory: Ephesians 6:1-3

Children, obey your parents in the Lord, for this is right. "Honor your father and mother"—which is the first commandment with a promise—"that it may go well with you and that you may enjoy long life on the earth." (NIV)

Children, obey your parents in the Lord, for this is right. Honor your father and mother (which is the first commandment with a promise), so that it may be well with you, and that you may live long on the earth. (NASB)

Children, obey your parents in the Lord, for this is right. "Honor your father and mother," which is the first commandment with promise: "That it may be well with you and you may live long on the earth." (NKJV)

Story Starter

Tyler's mom worked all morning to get the house cleaned up for the party. It was his birthday, and his friends were coming over. He wondered what wonderful presents he would get. He wanted to share his excitement with his mom, but then he realized that she was working so hard for him. He decided he wanted her to know, even before he got any presents, how much he appreciated what she was doing for him. How did Tyler honor his mom?

Notes
_____
_____
_____
_____
_____
_____
_____
_____

Our Family Way 4

Concerning AUTHORITIES in our family

We listen to correction and accept discipline with a submissive spirit.

Our Family Way 4

Concerning AUTHORITIES in our family

A → **Ask A Question**

R ⊻ **Read The Bible**

Day 1

Why should an Olympic athlete follow his coach's instructions and advice? What would happen if he didn't?

What would you be like if you were never disciplined or corrected? Better or worse?

Hebrews 12:7-11

The writer of Hebrews explains that God's discipline is as natural a part of life as is the discipline of a father. The key is submitting to it and learning from it. It is for our good.

Day 2

Think of all the ways that your parents can discipline you when you've disobeyed. Which ones work the best? Which don't work?

Create a family disciplinary code—identify family offenses and their punishments.

Proverbs 1:1-7

Solomon begins his book of wisdom by telling the reader what the proverbs are good for—attaining wisdom and discipline. Verse 7 is the theme for the entire book of Proverbs.

Day 3

How would you train a new puppy dog to follow your commands?

What are some things you really don't like to do, but when you make yourself do them, you like what you are able to do? to be kind? to be good?

Proverbs 3:11-12

Solomon instructs his sons concerning God's discipline, which he describes as an act of divine love just as a father's discipline is motivated by love and "delight" for his child.

Day 4

If you were a parent, how would you train your children not to touch electrical outlets? not to go into the street? to be kind? to be good?

Think of ten things you can learn now as a child that will help you when you are older.

Proverbs 4:14-19, 22:6

Proverbs is all about choosing between God's way, and the world's way...between wisdom, and foolishness. A child must be directed onto God's path through wisdom and discipline.

Day 5

You're lost in a dark cave, but you are not afraid because you brought everything you need. What do you have? (*guide, map, light*)

What would your life be like if your parents never instructed you? Why?

Proverbs 6:20-23

Solomon exhorts his sons to keep the commands and teachings they have learned at home, and to learn from their parents' discipline how to walk in the light.

e listen to correction and accept discipline with a submissive spirit.

 **Talk About It**

Speak To God

How does discipline help you "share" in God's holiness? How is it for our "good"? (10)

In what ways have you been "trained"? (11)

Based on this passage, how should you think about your parents' discipline?

Thank God for parents who will train you so your life can be pleasing to God.

Praise God that he disciplines you for your own good because he loves you.

Pray for good attitudes about discipline.

How many times is discipline mentioned?

List all the different benefits that Solomon attributes to his proverbs.

Why is the "fear of the Lord" so important? What is one called who does not fear God?

Pray that your parents will help you become wise through their discipline.

Ask God to help you understand what it means to "fear" him.

Tell God you want to follow and obey him.

In what ways does God "discipline" us and "rebuke" (or, correct) us as a Father?

In what ways could you "despise" or "resent" God's discipline and rebuke?

How should you think about his discipline?

Thank God for his love that motivates him to want the best for you.

Pray that God will soften your heart to receive his discipline and hear his rebuke.

Confess any sinful attitudes in your heart.

What are the two "paths" of life that we can choose? What are they like?

What is the "full light of day"? (4:18)

What is the "way" in which a "child" (or, youth) should go?

Pray that your father and mother will help you know and choose the path of life.

Thank God that your parents love you and train you to walk wisely.

Praise God for showing you the way of life.

How do you "bind" your parents' teachings to your heart and "fasten them [to] your neck"?

How are they a "lamp" and a "light"?

Why are the "corrections of discipline" equated with "the way to life"?

Thank God for parents who teach you and discipline you to guide you in life.

Ask God to help you always remember your parents' instruction and discipline.

Pray that you will stay on the way of life.

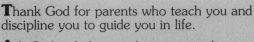

Learning the Way

We listen to correction and accept discipline with a submissive spirit.

Commentary

Biblical discipline is more than just correction of wrong behavior. It is also direction into right behavior. Both, though, require a willing submission to God, first, and to parents. A submissive spirit is a soft heart that will listen and respond.

Character: Submissive

Willingly accepting and following the authorities God has placed over my life.

Scripture Memory: Hebrews 12:11

No discipline seems pleasant at the time, but painful. Later on, however, it produces a harvest of righteousness and peace for those who have been trained by it. (NIV)

All discipline for the moment seems not to be joyful, but sorrowful; yet to those who have been trained by it, afterwards it yields the peaceful fruit of righteousness. (NASB)

Now no chastening seems to be joyful for the present, but grievous; nevertheless, afterward it yields the peaceable fruit of righteousness to those who have been trained by it. (NKJV)

Story Starter

A rainy day meant one thing to Holly...puddle jumping! She couldn't wait to splash and dash in the new puddles. "Just make sure," her dad instructed, "that you don't come into the house muddy and wet. Clean up first. Do you understand?" She blurted an excited, "Okay, Dad!" and shot outside. After an hour of running and jumping, an exhausted Holly thought, "I'm so tired. I'll bet I can sneak in the back door and no one will notice." But dad was right there. What should Holly's attitude be when her dad corrects her?

Notes

Our Family Way 5

Concerning RELATIONSHIPS in our family

We love one another, treating others with kindness, gentleness and respect.

Our Family Way 5

Concerning RELATIONSHIPS in our family

A
Ask A Question

R
Read The Bible

Day 1

If they never heard you say "I love you," how else would people know that you love your parents? your brothers and sisters?

What are ten ways to say "I love you" without speaking any words?

1 John 4:7-12

John, also called the "Apostle of love," explains the marks of true Christianity in his first epistle. The most important mark for believers—that we love one another.

Day 2

If you had been one of Jesus' closest disciples, what would you have expected or wanted him to say in his last hours with you?

If love was glue, who would be stuck to you? who would you be stuck to?

John 15:9-17

John recalls the words of Jesus to his disciples on their last night together before his crucifixion. The Lord's parting words were to love each other just as he had loved them.

Day 3

Have each family member boast about themselves for 30 seconds (time them). Talk about how it affects family unity and love.

What are the most loving things you have ever done? How did you feel?

1 Corinthians 13

Because of sinful pride about certain gifts, the Corinthian church was not unified. Paul reminds them that any spiritual gift is meaningless without love, which is the greatest gift.

Day 4

Have each family member say something loving about every other member. Talk about how it affects family unity and love.

With each piece of clothing being an act of love, describe getting dressed.

Colossians 3:12-14

Paul reminds the Colossian Christians that love for one another is the supreme goal for the body of Christ, the church. It is love that bonds and unifies believers as one in Christ.

Day 5

If acts of love were money, would people think you were rich or poor? Why?

If "do no harm to your neighbor" were the only law in America, describe what life might be like. Would that be enough law?

Romans 13:8-10

Paul concludes his letter to the Christians living in Rome by asserting that their highest responsibility is not to keep laws, but to love one another. Love fulfills the law of God.

24

*W*e love one another, treating others with kindness, gentleness and respect.

T Talk About It

S Speak To God

What are all the reasons John gives for why we should love one another?

How has God expressed his love for us? (9)

What does God's love for us motivate us to do? How is his love "made complete in us"?

Thank God for his love for us that sent Jesus, his Son, to die for our sins.

Praise God that we can know him and know his love, and be complete in him.

Pray to love others as Jesus loves them.

How does Jesus say they could show their love for him and one another? (10)

How can you "lay down your life" for your friends? for your family?

What is the "fruit" Jesus talks about? (16)

Thank God for Jesus, who laid down his life for you because he loves you so much.

Pray that you will show your love for God through your obedience of him.

Thank God for all those who love you.

What does Paul say love is? What does he say love is not?

Put your name in the place of "love." Does it describe you? Why, or why not?

Why is love greater than faith or hope? (13)

Ask God to help you see ways that you are not being loving in your family.

Ask God to help you love your family in a way that reflects the love of 1 Corinthians 13.

Pray through 1 Corinthians 13.

Describe an example from your family life of each "virtue" Paul says to put on.

What "grievances" in your family must be forgiven? How does God forgive?

What is "love"? *(feelings vs. actions)*

Thank God for the love of your father and mother for you.

Confess any grievances against others and ask for their forgiveness.

Pray for God's love to unite your family.

Why do we have a "continuing debt to love one another"? When is it fully paid? (8)

How does loving your neighbor fulfill all of God's commandments?

What does it mean to do "no harm"? (10)

Ask God to help you see those around you who need the love you can give.

Pray for those you know who are lonely and in need of love, and ask what you can do.

Pray for God's love to fill your heart.

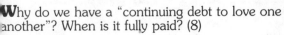

Learning the Way

Our Family Way 5 ~ Concerning RELATIONSHIPS in our family

We love one another, treating others with kindness, gentleness and respect.

Commentary

How we treat others reveals whether or not we truly love them. Love is the highest virtue in Scripture, the source of all other relational virtues. You don't love just because you "feel" loving, but because you choose to "act" in a loving way.

Character: Love

Wanting only the best for others and showing it in how I treat them and speak to them.

Scripture Memory: 1 John 4:11-12

Dear friends, since God so loved us, we also ought to love one another. No one has ever seen God; but if we love one another, God lives in us and his love is made complete in us. (NIV)

Beloved, if God so loved us, we also ought to love one another. No one has seen God at any time; if we love one another, God abides in us, and His love is perfected in us. (NASB)

Beloved, if God so loved us, we also ought to love one another. No one has seen God at any time. If we love one another, God abides in us and His love has been perfected in us. (NKJV)

Story Starter

Devon loved Saturdays with his friend, Nick. This particular one was a perfect day to be outside, and he looked forward to a day of doing "boy things" with his best pal—biking, exploring, and "stuff like that." They were just getting warmed up by playing some catch in the backyard. That's when Devon's little sister Summer came outside and saw the two boys. "Can I play, too?" she asked. Though tempted to say she was too little, Devon remembered the times his big brother had let him play, too. What do you think he said to her?

Notes

Our Family Way 6

Concerning RELATIONSHIPS in our family

We serve one another, humbly thinking of the needs of others first.

Our Family Way 6

Concerning RELATIONSHIPS in our family

A

Ask A Question

R

Read The Bible

Day 1

If you had your own personal servant, how would you expect to be treated? How would you expect not to be treated?

Think of ten specific ways that you could serve your mother today?

Mark 10:35-45

When the disciples begin to dispute with each other about who should be honored more, Jesus rebukes them and says that to become great one must sacrifice all to serve others.

Day 2

Vote on "Best Family Servant" awards in different categories—dishes, picking up toys, offering the last cookie, and others.

Describe a time when someone was looking out for you and helped you unexpectedly.

Philippians 2:1-4

Paul reminds the believers at Philippi, his favorite church, that their highest purpose as a church is to be unified—to be one in the Spirit. That only comes through humility and service.

Day 3

If you were selected to be the leader of a new country, which leaders out of history would you want to ask for advice? Why?

If you were going to be an insect for a day, what kind would you be? Why?

Philippians 2:5-11

Paul exhorts the Philippians to model their attitude after the Lord Jesus, who humbled himself to become a servant on our behalf in obedience to God, and died on a cross.

Day 4

In turn, have each family member identify and describe every other person's most outstanding skills, talents, and qualities.

Decide what part of a physical body each family member best represents.

Romans 12:3-5

After exhorting the Roman Christians to offer themselves in service to God, Paul goes on to admonish them that only humility and faith will unify them as the body of Christ.

Day 5

If you could go shopping to "clothe yourself with humility," what kind of outfit would you buy? Describe each piece.

What would you think about a child who had an adult body? Why?

1 Peter 5:5-7

Peter instructs believers to be submissive to those who are older, and for everyone to be humble with one another. God is against the proud, but gives grace to the humble.

We serve one another, humbly thinking of the needs of others first.

Talk About It

Speak To God

What did James and John want? What was the "glory" of Christ they anticipated? (37)

Why were the other disciples upset? (41)

What did Jesus say was the key to greatness? Why is that still true today?

Pray that you will become great in God's kingdom by humbly serving others.

Thank God for those you know in ministry who are servants for his kingdom.

Pray for the leaders of your church.

What does Paul say would make him the happiest to hear about the church? (2)

What would keep you from having a humble attitude toward other believers?

What does it mean to "look" to others? (4)

Pray that your family will be unified as Paul wanted the Philippian family to be.

Confess any "selfish ambition" or "vain conceit" or any other kind of sinful pride.

Pray for humility of mind and heart.

How is Jesus' attitude an example of humility, sacrifice, and service?

Jesus could have come to earth as a ruler, so why did he come as a servant?

How can your attitude be more like Jesus'?

Thank God for what Jesus did for you in humbling himself to become a servant.

Praise him because his name is now the most important name in all creation.

Pray that you can become like Jesus.

What kind of attitude should believers have of themselves? How does "grace" help? (3)

How can one "think...with sober judgment"?

How is your own body a picture of how the church body works together? the family?

Pray for the "sober judgment" that will help you, by faith, stay humble.

Praise God for the body of Christ.

Pray that every member of your family will know they are important.

Why does Peter single out "young men" to talk about submission and humility?

Why is "grace" only for the humble?

What does Paul say to do if you want to be honored and recognized?

Thank God that his grace and care is available to the humble of heart.

Pray that God would give you the grace to be a humble servant to all in your family, whatever your age may be.

Learning the Way

Our Family Way 6 ~ Concerning RELATIONSHIPS in our family

We serve one another, humbly thinking of the needs of others first.

Commentary

Jesus came not to be served, but to serve, and to humbly give his life to save ours. He simply wants us to follow his example. Christ's sacrifice on the cross is the supreme example of the kind of humility we are to have toward one another.

Character: Service

Doing for others without expecting them to do anything for me in return.

Scripture Memory: Mark 10:44-45

...whoever wants to become great among you must be your servant, and whoever wants to be first must be slave of all. For even the Son of Man did not come to be served, but to serve, and to give his life as a ransom for many. (NIV)

...and whoever wishes to be first among you shall be slave of all. "For even the Son of Man did not come to be served, but to serve, and to give His life a ransom for many." (NASB)

...whoever desires to become great among you shall be your servant. And whoever of you desires to be first shall be slave of all. For even the Son of Man did not come to be served, but to serve, and to give His life a ransom for many. (NKJV)

Story Starter

Whatever Lilly did, she did it with all her energy. She had played soccer that morning, and had been bicycling around the neighborhood that afternoon. She was so tired. Her mother had already asked Lilly three times to bring all her dirty laundry downstairs so she could wash. Lilly thought she could lay down for just a second, but soon she was asleep, surrounded by dirty clothes. Andrew could have awakened her and told her that their mother was still waiting, but he didn't. What did he do instead, and why did he do it?

Notes

We encourage one another, using only *words* that build up and bless others.

Our Family Way 7

Concerning RELATIONSHIPS in our family

A ➡ Ask A Question

R Read The Bible

Day 1

If your words became bricks after they left your mouth, what kind of building would you be able to build with them?

Think of at least ten words that make you feel good when they're about you.

Ephesians 4:29-32

Paul, having shown his readers their position in Christ in chapters 1-3, goes on to tell them how to live in Christ in light of that position, and how to use words to build up others.

Day 2

Your basketball team has played the first half very poorly and you are losing. You are the coach—what do you say?

Describe a time someone encouraged you secretly. How did it make you feel?

Hebrews 10:23-25

The author of Hebrews encourages believers, scattered from Jerusalem, to persevere in their newfound faith, and to encourage one another to live out that faith every day.

Day 3

Sing an "Amen" chorus loudly with off-pitch disharmony. Then sing it in unison and with harmony. What is the difference?

You will inherit $1.00 for every kind word you've spoken. Will you be rich?

1 Peter 3:8-12

Peter instructs his readers to live in unity and love, to persevere in their faith, to do good, and to be a blessing to one another in order to live harmoniously and peacefully.

Day 4

Have each person create a melody and sing the memory verse to the family.

In turn, have each family member say one thing they are thankful for about every other family member. Try not to repeat.

Colossians 3:15-17

The Colossian church was vulnerable to divisiveness, so Paul instructs them to set aside the old way of life, and to put on the new self in Christ in order to live in peace and love.

Day 5

Name ten words that stab like a sword; name ten words that soothe like a salve.

Role play "gentle answers" to possible attitudes: "You're not my friend." "You're not that good at that." "Mine is better."

Proverbs 12:18; 15:1, 23; 16:24

The tongue is a common topic of Proverbs, particularly its misuse. These four Proverbs are representative of many others of the positive purpose and power of the tongue.

We encourage one another, using only words that build up and bless others.

T Talk About It

What is "unwholesome talk"? What kind of talk "builds up" and "benefits" others? (29)

If you were always "kind," "compassionate" and "forgiving," how would it change you? What actions must you "get rid of"?

What is the "hope we profess"?

What does it mean to "spur one another on toward love and good deeds"?

How does "meeting together," or fellowship, encourage you as a Christian?

What does it mean to "live in harmony"?

What does it mean to respond to "evil" or "insult" with a "blessing"? Think of an example.

According to verses 10-12, why should we do what is described in verses 8-9?

How do you "let the peace of Christ rule in your hearts"? What else rules there?

How do you "let the word of Christ dwell in you richly"? What do you do with it?

Why is being "thankful" so important?

What are "reckless words"? What is a "harsh word"? What effect do they have?

How can words bring "healing"? How can they "turn away wrath"?

How do your words reflect these verses?

S Speak To God

Pray that God will help you use only words that build up and benefit others.

Confess any unwholesome talk or anger. Ask forgiveness if you have offended anyone with your words or attitudes.

Thank God for our hope of eternal life.

Ask God to help you be an encourager in your family through love and deed.

Thank God for those who encourage you and spur you on as a Christian.

Pray that your family would be known for its "harmony" and spirit of peace.

Thank God that his eyes are on you.

Ask God to help you be a blessing to others, even when they insult you.

Pray that the peace of Christ would rule in your family's hearts today.

Pray that the Bible will be a part of everything you do as a family.

Thank God for Jesus and the Bible.

Confess any "reckless" or "harsh" words you may have spoken to your family.

Ask God to help you control your words so that they bring healing to others.

Pray that your words will honor God.

Learning the Way

Our Family Way 7 ~ Concerning RELATIONSHIPS in our family

We encourage one another, using only words that build up and bless others.

Commentary

Encouragement is a willful act of love. It is easy to "tear down" a person's spirit with careless and hurtful words. To "build up" a person means thinking carefully about not only what to say, but how to say it. You cannot encourage others accidentally.

Character: Encouragement

Speaking words to others that build them up and lift them up in the Lord.

Scripture Memory: Ephesians 4:29

Do not let any unwholesome talk come out of your mouths, but only what is helpful for building others up according to their needs, that it may benefit those who listen. (NIV)

Let no unwholesome word proceed from your mouth, but only such a word as is good for edification according to the need of the moment, so that it will give grace to those who hear. (NASB)

Let no corrupt communication proceed out of your mouth, but what is good for necessary edification, that it may impart grace to the hearers. (NKJV)

Story Starter

Everyone always marveled at Darla's chocolate cakes. She had become quite the young baker, and had already won several prizes at the county fair and other places. Her younger cousin, Katie, was just beginning, and didn't know how to bake a cake. But she was so excited by the Participation ribbon she received for her cupcakes at the county fair. Even though Darla had won first place, she didn't say anything about it and fussed over Katie's ribbon. What do you think Darla said to Katie that made her smile?

Notes _____

_____

_____

_____

_____

_____

_____

_____

Our Family Way 8

Concerning RELATIONSHIPS in our family

We forgive one another, covering an offense with love when wronged or hurt.

Our Family Way 8

Concerning RELATIONSHIPS in our family

A — Ask A Question

R — Read The Bible

Day 1

Think of ten things that you might have to forgive one another for during a normal day at home. Be general, not personal.

If you painted a picture of forgiveness, what would it look like? What colors?

Colossians 3:12-14

In the midst of instructing the Colossians about the godly virtues and about love, Paul reminds them that forgiveness is at the heart of the gospel, so they should forgive, too.

Day 2

Imagine a friend took your new bike without your permission and wrecked it. How specifically would you pray for them?

If forgiveness were a thing you could hold, what would it look like? feel like?

Matthew 6:9-15

In this portion of the Sermon on the Mount, Jesus instructs his followers how to pray, and then reminds them that forgiveness of others is the first priority in prayer.

Day 3

Imagine your brother or sister decided to pester you every seven minutes one day. How long would you endure it?

If forgiveness cleans up a pile of dirty clothes, describe how big your pile is each day?

Matthew 18:21-35

An offender needed to be forgiven only three times in Jesus' day. Peter tries to sound noble, but he surely did not expect what Jesus would say, or the parable he told.

Day 4

When you meet someone new, what clues can you look for in their life to determine whether or not they really love God?

What things have you learned to do because someone first showed you how?

1 John 4:19-21

John reflects the teachings of Jesus about loving our fellow Christians. The mark of a Christian is love for other believers, and where there is hate, he says, there is no love.

Day 5

If you knew that Jesus would return in one year, what would you do? How would it change your relationships with others?

What about you would you like others to cover and hide with an invisible blanket?

1 Peter 4:7-8

Peter concludes his letter with a series of short exhortations about the Christian life. As with Paul's teaching, love is the Christian's most important responsibility.

We forgive one another, covering an offense with love when wronged or hurt.

Talk About It

Speak To God

What does it mean to "bear with each other"? How do you do that at home?

What are the kinds of "grievances," or complaints, that Paul refers to?

What has Jesus forgiven in your life?

Thank the Lord for his forgiveness of all your sins by his death on the cross.

Confess any ways you have offended others, or grudges you are holding onto wrongly.

Ask God for a forgiving heart.

Observe the attention first to heavenly things (9-10) and then to earthly things (11-13).

What "debts" (sins) do we have each day that need God's forgiveness?

Why is forgiveness so important?

Thank God for all the ways he cares for and protects you every day.

Confess and ask God to forgive your sins.

Consider if you need to forgive others before God for their sins against you.

What was Peter really asking? What is the point of Jesus' answer?

What is the point of the parable for Peter?

What will keep you from becoming like the unmerciful servant?

Thank God that there is no limit to his forgiveness of sins, that it won't run out.

Praise God that you have been forgiven a debt you could not repay (your sin).

Pray for a forgiving heart.

Why is someone a liar if they hate their "brother" but say they love God? (20)

What is the relationship between hate, love, and forgiveness?

How can you love a God you don't see?

Thank God that he loved you first, and that you can love him because of Christ.

Ask God to help you love your family and other Christians.

Pray for eyes in your heart to see God.

Is the "end of all things" still near? If so, what then should characterize our lives?

How do you love "deeply"? (*forgive*)

What does Peter see as the fruit of godly love? (*forgiveness*)

Pray that you can live every day as though Christ might return that day.

Ask God to give you a deep love for your family, and spirit of forgiveness.

Thank him that his love covers your sin.

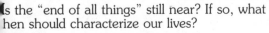

Learning the Way

Our Family Way 8 ~ Concerning RELATIONSHIPS in our family

We forgive one another, covering an offense with love when wronged or hurt.

Commentary

Our sins are forgiven by God, so he wants us to forgive others when they sin against us. Forgiveness may not always mean forgetting a wrong, but it does mean choosing not to remember it. We cover others' sins just like Jesus does ours.

Character: Forgiveness

Treating someone who has offended me as though I had never been hurt.

Scripture Memory: Colossians 3:13

Bear with each other and forgive whatever grievances you may have against one another. Forgive as the Lord forgave you. (NIV)

...bearing with one another, and forgiving each other, whoever has a complaint against anyone; just as the Lord forgave you, so also should you. (NASB)

...bearing with one another, and forgiving one another, if anyone has a complaint against another; even as Christ forgave you, so you also must do. (NKJV)

Story Starter

Matthew couldn't resist picking up his brother's cool new model airplane. Soon, he was a fearless pilot zooming his aircraft all around his brother's room. He didn't see their dog, Missy, come into the room. She wanted to play, too! But with his eyes to the skies, Matthew tripped over the dog and he and the model plane went crashing to earth on the floor. It was broken. Matthew felt awful when he showed the broken model to Christopher. What do you think Christopher's response should be?

Notes _____

_____

_____

_____

_____

_____

_____

_____

Our Family Way 9

Concerning POSSESSIONS in our family

We are thankful to God for what we have, whether it is a little or a lot.

Our Family Way 9

Concerning POSSESSIONS in our family

A → *Ask A Question*

R ⩔ *Read The Bible*

Day 1

What things have you complained about to others recently? How could those things be turned into "thanks" to God?

For one minute, say as many things that you can think of to give thanks for.

1 Thessalonians 5:16-18

Paul wrote to the Thessalonian church to encourage them to remain faithful. In a series of closing exhortations, he reminds them of key spiritual priorities for believers.

Day 2

If you really had to, what things could you live without? What things do you think that you simply must have, no matter what?

If you were a bird, what kinds of foods would you want God to feed you with?

Matthew 6:25-27

Jesus teaches his disciples and the multitudes in his Sermon on the Mount. He pointed to birds flying by in the fields of Galilee to illustrate his teaching about God's provision.

Day 3

If all you could own was one small suitcase full of clothes, what pieces of clothing would you pack? What would you leave out?

If you were a wildflower, what colors would you want God to clothe you in?

Matthew 6:28-30

As Jesus continues his Sermon on the Mount, he turns his listeners' attention to the colorful, abundant wildflowers that were surely all around them in the rolling hills and fields.

Day 4

What things do you think about or worry about instead of thinking about God?

If a king gave you the choice of having either glory and honor, or power and wealth, which would you choose? Why?

Matthew 6:31-34

As Jesus continues his Sermon on the Mount, he concludes his thoughts on "worry" by reminding his hearers what is really important in this life—his kingdom and righteousness.

Day 5

Would you rather be poor and happy, or rich and unhappy? Why?

If you were poor, what things would you be most thankful for? If you were rich, what things would you thank God for?

James 1:9-11

James, the brother of Jesus, instructs and exhorts his readers, probably mostly Jewish Christians, in godly wisdom (similar to Proverbs) and in how to live the Christian life.

We are thankful to God for what we have, whether it is a little or a lot.

T Talk About It

S Speak To God

How can you be joyful "always" (at all times)? How can you pray "continually"?

How can you give thanks in "all circumstances"? Are there any exceptions?

How are these "God's will" for you?

Pray for a heart of constant joyfulness.

Ask God to help you become a persistent prayer all day long.

Thank God for both the blessings and the difficulties in His will for your life.

What does Jesus say we should not "worry" about? What happens when we worry?

What is the "life" that Jesus means? (25b)

What do the "birds of the air" teach you about what is important in life?

Praise God that he knows about and meets all your basic needs in life.

Pray that God will help you see how much he cares for you, even in little ways.

Thank Jesus for your life in him.

What does Jesus mean, "why do you worry about clothes"? Do we?

What do wildflowers teach you about God's provision for your needs? (30)

How, exactly, will God "clothe you"?

Thank God that He provides clothes to keep you covered and warm.

Praise God for his love and his care for you and your family's needs.

Confess it if you "worry about clothes."

Who are "pagans" and what do they do?

How can you "seek first his kingdom and righteousness"? What are those?

What "things" will be given to you "as well" when you seek God's kingdom?

Thank God that he has revealed his kingdom and his righteousness to you in the Bible.

Ask the Father to help you seek after him with all your heart.

Praise him for his sovereign care.

What attitude should the poor man have? Why is his life called a "high position"?

What attitude should the rich man have? Why is his life called a "low position"?

Which one is better? Why?

Thank God for whatever you have as a family, whether it is much or little.

Pray for a humble spirit and a godly attitude about your present circumstances, whether you are rich or poor.

Learning the Way

Our Family Way 9 ~ Concerning POSSESSIONS in our family

We are thankful to God for what we have, whether it is a little or a lot.

Commentary

When we are thankful for what God gives us, we are telling him we trust him as our Heavenly Father. Regardless of how he has blessed us, he is looking for a thankful attitude in our hearts. He knows gratitude will change our hearts.

Character: Thankfulness

Being glad and grateful for my life, and showing it.

Scripture Memory: 1 Thessalonians 5:16-18

Be joyful always; pray continually; give thanks in all circumstances, for this is God's will for you in Christ Jesus. (NIV)

Rejoice always; pray without ceasing; in everything give thanks; for this is God's will for you in Christ Jesus. (NASB)

Rejoice always, pray without ceasing, in everything give thanks; for this is the will of God in Christ Jesus for you. (NKJV)

Story Starter

Kendall and her family never wanted to leave their home in the country. It was the only home she had known. But her father had to take a new job in the city, so they reluctantly moved into a small home in an older neighborhood closer to his work. Kendall was tempted at first to be very sad, and to not like anything about the new home. But her mother helped her find new things to thank God for. One day when she was missing the country, a little kitty wandered into the yard. She named it Kali and thanked God for it. What helped Kendall to be happy in her new home?

Notes

Our Family Way 10

Concerning POSSESSIONS in our family

We are content with what we have, not coveting what others have.

Our Family Way 10

Concerning POSSESSIONS in our family

Ask A Question

Read The Bible

Day 1

Satan has set many traps along the roadside of life. What kind of "bait" does he use to lure you off God's path of life?

What different kinds of fruit grow on the "love of money" tree? Are they sweet?

1 Timothy 6:6-10

Paul instructs his young disciple, Timothy, about how to lead the growing church. He warns him about the temptations of wealth and the importance of godliness and contentment.

Day 2

If a thief broke into your house, what things could he steal that would break your heart? What would you not miss?

Role play what God and Money might say to you to try to win your allegiance. Who wins?

Matthew 6:19-24

In his Sermon on the Mount, Jesus instructs his disciples and followers that the heart can be committed either to the things of God or to the things of the world, but not to both.

Day 3

Imagine that you are in a foreign land with no money, surrounded by strangers. What would you think? What would you do?

What things can you do with God's strength that you cannot do without it?

Philippians 4:10-13

Paul writes from "house arrest" in Rome to thank the Philippian church for a financial gift. He tells them he has learned to be content in Christ whether he has a little or a lot.

Day 4

What things do you have that someone else might want? What would you say to someone who wrongly coveted them?

Have you ever wanted something so badly it bothered you? What did you do?

Exodus 20:17

The tenth of the Ten Commandments given by God to the people of Israel at Mt. Sinai is an issue of the heart—don't wrongly desire what isn't yours. Coveting is a "top ten" sin.

Day 5

If there was a scripture that said "Keep yourself free from the love of toys," what would you do to obey it?

If you knew God would help you, what would you dare to do with your life?

Hebrews 13:5-6

As the writer of Hebrews concludes his letter, he admonishes his readers to trust in God, not in money or things. He quotes the Old Testament to remind them it is on the heart of God.

We are content with what we have, not coveting what others have.

T **Talk About It**

S **Speak To God**

What is the "gain" (value) of contentment?

Why is the desire to be rich a "trap" that leads to ruin and destruction"? (9)

What kinds of "evil" grow from the "root" Paul calls the "love of money"? (10)

Tell God that you desire to be a godly, contented Christian more than desiring wealth.

Pray that God will protect your heart from the evils of the love of money.

Thank God for what you have.

What are "treasures on earth"? What are "treasures in heaven"?

What does it mean for your eyes to be "good" or "bad"? What is the "light"?

Why can you not serve two "masters"?

Ask God to show you his heavenly treasures for your heart to pursue.

Tell God you're sorry if you have set your heart on things rather than on him.

Set your heart on God with praise.

Why does Paul "rejoice greatly in the Lord"?

How did Paul "learn" to be content? Did God always meet all of his needs?

What was the "secret" Paul learned? How did God's "strength" help him? (13)

Rejoice in the Lord for material blessings you have from God as a family.

Ask God to help you learn the secret of "being content" in all circumstances.

Pray for strength to be content.

How is the last commandment, "do not covet," different from the first nine? (*motive*)

Who is "your neighbor"? What other things can be wrongly coveted?

When, if ever, is "coveting" acceptable?

Ask God to reveal any things that belong to others that you might be coveting.

Pray for a heart that is content with what you have, and that does not covet.

Pray for godly desires and wants.

What can a Christian do to keep his life "free from the love of money"?

What Bible truth allows you to always be content, no matter what you have or lack?

What is your reason for "confidence"? (6)

Pray that God will help you keep your heart free from the "love of money."

Thank God that he will always be with you, no matter what your circumstances.

Praise God for taking care of you.

Learning the Way

Our Family Way 10 ~ Concerning POSSESSIONS in our family

We are content with what we have, not coveting what others have.

Commentary

Someone, somewhere, sometime will always have more than you do. Contentedness is learning to say, "That's okay. I have enough." Like thankfulness, contentedness is an expression of trust in God, and in his ability to provide all that we need.

Character: Contentment

Deciding to be happy with my circumstances, whatever they may be.

Scripture Memory: 1 Timothy 6:6-8

But godliness with contentment is great gain. For we brought nothing into the world, and we can take nothing out of it. But if we have food and clothing, we will be content with that. (NIV)

But godliness actually is a means of great gain when accompanied by contentment. For we have brought nothing into the world, so we cannot take anything out of it either. If we have food and covering, with these we shall be content. (NASB)

But godliness with contentment is great gain. For we brought nothing into this world, and it is certain we can carry nothing out. And having food and clothing, with these we shall be content. (NKJV)

Story Starter

All the kids in the neighborhood looked forward to the Fourth of July bike parade to show off their decorated bicycles. Matthew's bike, a hand-me-down, was old, starting to rust, and was even too small for him. Still, he decided he would put his whole heart into decorating it. But just as he was finishing up, Jonathan came over to show Matthew his brand new bike. It was so cool! Matthew admired Jonathan's bike, and then showed him how he was decorating his old bike. What kept Matthew from being jealous?

Notes

_____

_____

_____

_____

_____

_____

_____

_____

Our Family Way 11

Concerning POSSESSIONS in our family

We are generous with what we have, sharing freely with others.

Our Family Way 11

Concerning POSSESSIONS in our family

A — Ask A Question

R — Read The Bible

Day 1

You're down to your last sack of seeds. Do you keep some back just in case, or do you plant them all? Why?

Role-play both a "reluctant" and a "cheerful" giver. Which do you prefer? Why?

2 Corinthians 9:6-11

As a follow-up to his first letter, Paul writes to the Corinthian Christians to defend his questioned apostleship, and to urge them to give money generously for the poor in Jerusalem.

Day 2

Imagine you just received an unexpected gift of ten million dollars. How would it change your life? What would you do with it?

How much is in your spiritual bank account from deposits of good deeds?

1 Timothy 6:17-19

Paul instructs his young disciple, Timothy, about how to lead the growing church. In closing, he counsels him on how to admonish and instruct Christians who are wealthy.

Day 3

Identify individuals or groups of poor or unfortunate people that your family could help in some way. Talk about how.

If you were poor, what "gift" would encourage you the most? Why?

Psalm 112

The psalmist describes the "blessed" man, who has much and fears the Lord. He trusts God and lives righteously, which is evident in his generosity and concern for the poor.

Day 4

If you sold everything you own to give to the poor, would you then be poor? What riches and assets would you still have?

What Christian men and women do you really admire? What is their "treasure"?

Luke 12:32-34

In the midst of teaching the multitudes who are following him, Jesus turns to address his disciples personally about money, possessions, the heart, and the kingdom of God.

Day 5

If you received a $10 gift, how much would you give to God's work? What about $100? $1,000?

How much extra spending money do you have right now? What would make you be willing to give all of it to God's work?

Mark 12:41-44

Jesus often taught his followers in the temple courts in Jerusalem. On this occasion, he draws his disciples' attention to a poor widow who has come to make her offering.

We are generous with what we have, sharing freely with others.

Talk About It

Speak To God

What should be the motivation of your heart for giving to God's work? Why?	Pray that God will give you a generous heart for helping others in his name.
What does God give in return? (8)	Pray that, by his grace, you can be "rich in every way" so you can give more.
What is the ultimate fruit of giving generously and cheerfully? (10-11)	Thank God for your blessings.

What heart attitudes must you be careful to resist you have a lot of money?	Examine your heart for any signs of arrogance or pride related to money.
What should you do, if you are rich, to be sure you are wealthy spiritually as well?	Ask God to reveal to you ways for you to be generous, and rich in good works.
What is "the life that is truly life"? (19)	Thank God for your spiritual riches.

What are the main characteristics of the man described in this psalm? (2-5)	Pray through this psalm for your family.
How certain is his trust in God? (6-8)	Pray that God will help you see your money from the perspective of eternity.
What is it about this man's life that will bring him honor in eternity? (9)	Ask God to give you a spirit of grace and generosity for the poor and needy.

What is the "kingdom" God has given to us? Why should that allay our fears?	Thank God that his kingdom is eternal, not just for a few years of this earthly life.
What does Jesus mean when he says to pursue purses... that will not wear out"?	Ask God to help you make deposits in your heavenly bank account by giving up some things so you have more to give to the poor.
How can your heart be in heaven? (34)	

Was it easy or difficult for the rich people to give large amounts"? Why?	Talk with God about your giving, especially if it always seems pretty easy to give.
Was it easy or difficult for the poor widow to give less than a penny? Why?	Pray that he will help you become a more generous giver to his work.
Why does Jesus praise the widow? (44)	Tell God that all you have belongs to him.

49

Learning the Way

Our Family Way 11 ~ Concerning POSSESSIONS in our family

We are generous with what we have, sharing freely with others.

Commentary

Generosity is the outward expression of thankfulness and contentedness. It is a heart attitude that says, "God has generously blessed me, so I want to generously bless you." Generosity is holding things and money loosely, in open hands before God.

Character: Generosity

Happily sharing with others all that God has given to me.

Scripture Memory: 2 Corinthians 9:7

Each man should give what he has decided in his heart to give, not reluctantly or under compulsion, for God loves a cheerful giver. (NIV)

Each one must do just as he has purposed in his heart, not grudgingly or under compulsion, for God loves a cheerful giver. (NASB)

So let each one give as he purposes in his heart, not grudgingly or of necessity; for God loves a cheerful giver. (NKJV)

Story Starter

Mom declared it "Giveaway Saturday." She stood in the middle of the family room by a big, empty box and said, "Ask God if there are any things you have that others less fortunate might enjoy." Robert went through his things and found some toys and baseball gear he really liked, but wasn't using very much. Meredith found a coat she hated to part with, but sensed God wanted her to give it away. They remembered the children they had met at the homeless shelter the Christmas before, and decided to donate even a few more things from their rooms. How were they being generous?

Notes

Our Family Way 12

Concerning POSSESSIONS in our family

We take care of what we have, using it wisely and responsibly.

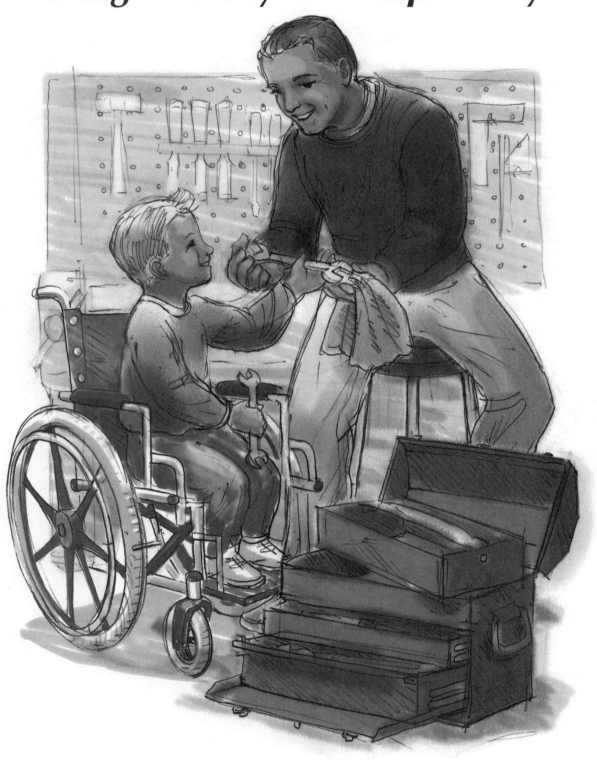

Our Family Way 12

Concerning POSSESSIONS in our family

Ask A Question

Read The Bible

Day 1

If the king made you manager of the royal treasury, how would you take care of it, and help to increase it wisely?

Who is the shrewdest person you know when it comes to money? Why are they?

Luke 16: 1-13 (or, 10-13)

Jesus commends the "unrighteous manager" in this difficult parable for being shrewd in dealing with wealth, probably by reducing debts by the unjust interest due to him.

Day 2

Imagine you are the head servant in a rich man's home. How would you live if the man went away for a whole year?

If Jesus returned today, would he call you a "faithful servant"? Why?

Matthew 24:45-51

Jesus exhorts his disciples to be ready when he returns. He tells several parables to illustrate the need to be prepared and faithful, and to be found doing his work on his return.

Day 3

You have been asked to build the new church pulpit. Should you use free scrap wood, or expensive new wood. Why?

What do you own that could be used by your church? Have you taken care of it?

Exodus 35:20-29

Moses comes down from Mt. Sinai after 40 days and begins to instruct the people. They willingly respond to God's command to build a tabernacle for his presence and worship.

Day 4

If your church burned down, what could you give, or sell, to help in rebuilding it?

What is something that you take very good care of because you want to keep it for a long time? How do you care for it?

1 Chronicles 29:14-19

David thanks God for the people of Israel who generously gave out of their possessions to help finance the building of the temple in Jerusalem. He prays, too, for Solomon.

Day 5

If you knew Jesus was looking, would you take better care of yours and your family's belongings? How? Why?

What is your most prized possession? How do you care for it? Why?

Proverbs 3:1-10

In the first nine chapters of Proverbs, Solomon instructs his sons concerning both the responsibilities and the benefits of trusting God and living wisely. Money is always an issue.

We take care of what we have, using it wisely and responsibly.

Talk About It

Speak To God

Assuming his actions were acceptable, why did the master call the manager shrewd?

Restate verses 10-12 in the form of a principle or rule that you can follow.

How should you think about money? (13)

Who is the faithful "servant" in this parable? the "master"? the "household"?

How will the master reward faithfulness in his servant? (47) unfaithfulness? (51)

How can you be a faithful servant? (46)

What was to be the motivation to give to the creation of the tabernacle? Why? (21)

What did the people give?

Were these precious, cared-for things, or discards? What's the difference?

What is David's response to the gifts?

Who does he say the gifts are really from? Why does he say that? (16)

Why is he so concerned about his motives and about integrity? Why should you be?

What brings "favor and good repute" in the eyes of God and man? (1-4)

How does the wise man live and make decisions? (5-8)

How does he view his wealth? (9-10)

Pray that God will protect you from making unwise decisions about money.

Pray that God will help you to be both wise and shrewd with your money.

Decide to be trustworthy and honest.

Tell God that you want to be found to be his "faithful servant" when he returns.

Ask God to help you use your life in a way that will honor him.

Pray that your family will all be faithful.

Pray that God would help you to be generous in giving to his work.

Ask God to show you if there are some good things you have that might be used to help other people or your church ministry.

Acknowledge as a family that all you have is from God and belongs to God.

Ask for integrity and the right heart motives in using what God has given you.

Pray that you will be a faithful servant.

Tell God you desire to live a life that is characterized by love and faithfulness.

Express your willingness to rely on him, not on your own wisdom, to be the kind of wise steward he wants you to be.

Learning the Way

Our Family Way 12 ~ Concerning POSSESSIONS in our family

We take care of what we have, using it wisely and responsibly.

Commentary

We never really "own" anything in this life. All that we have is from God, and he wants us to be good stewards, or managers, of whatever he has allowed us to enjoy. We take care of it because we know that, ultimately, it belongs to him.

Character: Stewardship

Using wisely everything that God has given to me— my time, my talents and my treasures.

Scripture Memory: Luke 16:10

Whoever can be trusted with very little can also be trusted with much, and whoever is dishonest with very little will also be dishonest with much. (NIV)

He who is faithful in a very little thing is faithful also in much; and he who is unrighteous in a very little thing is unrighteous also in much. (NASB)

He who is faithful in what is least is faithful also in much; and he who is unjust in what is least is unjust also in much. (NKJV)

Story Starter

Chase loved it when he got to spend the weekend at his uncle's house. Uncle Jimmy knew all about fixing things. Chase was good with his hands and wanted to learn all he could about using tools. His uncle told him, "You may use any of my tools. All I ask is that you put them away when you finish with them." Chase borrowed a wrench to tighten a bolt on his wheelchair when his aunt called out, "Milk and cookies!" He looked at his uncle and said, "Let's put up the tools first!" How do you think Uncle Jimmy felt?

Notes _____

_____

_____

_____

_____

_____

_____

_____

Our Family Way 13

Concerning WORK in our family

We are diligent to complete a task promptly and thoroughly when asked.

Our Family Way 13

Concerning WORK in our family

Ask A Question

Read The Bible

Day 1

Using all the letters in "diligent," think of at least eight words that describe a diligent person (ex., "d" for determined).

Using all the letters in "sluggard," do the same for the lazy person.

Proverbs 13:4, 10:4, 21:5

Many of the teachings in the book of Proverbs deal with the choice between man's foolish ways and God's wise ways. One's attitude toward work can reveal foolishness or wisdom.

Day 2

What is something you've done that you really did "with all your might"? How much effort or time did it take? Were you proud of it?

Would you rather work hard and be rewarded, or not work and be left alone?

Ecclesiastes 9:10, 11:6

The "Teacher" (traditionally seen as Solomon) examines life and reflects on the wisdom he has learned "under the sun." His conclusion: life is meaningless and empty without God.

Day 3

What has God made you good at? How can you use that skill for God as you grow up? How can you use it right now?

You are given $10, but you can keep it only if you turn it into $20. What would you do?

Matthew 25:14-30

Although the "talents" (money) in this parable really represent knowledge of God's kingdom, the underlying principles can also be applied to how we manage our lives and abilities.

Day 4

If you were a household servant in Jesus' day (a slave), what would you do to demonstrate your diligence to you master?

If you were a master, how would you know if your servant was being diligent?

Ephesians 6:5-9

Paul instructs slaves and masters of his day how to relate to one another. His advice to household servants still rings true to us today as servants of our Master, Jesus Christ.

Day 5

Think of three people you know that you would describe as being diligent in their Christian faith. Why did you choose them?

What are five ways you can become a more diligent Christian today?

Hebrews 6:9-12

Many Jews who had become Christians were turning back to the false security of sacrifices and temple worship. The writer of Hebrews exhorts them to maintain a diligent faith.

We are diligent to complete a task promptly and thoroughly when asked.

Talk About It

Speak To God

Why are the sluggard's desires unsatisfied and the diligent person's satisfied?

What are the rewards of "diligent hands"?

What is the relationship between diligence and money? Is that good? Why?

Tell God your desires and wants.

Ask him to strengthen your diligence so your godly desires will be satisfied.

Pray that God will help you to be a diligent worker to help your family.

Why should you do everything "with all your might"? Why not just be lazy? (9:10)

Is it ever okay to stop being diligent about life and opportunities? Why, or why not?

How can you be diligent "at evening"?

Talk to God about things in your life you want to begin to do "with all your might."

Ask God to help you be diligent all day long, not just when you feel like it.

Pray that you can make your life count.

What is Jesus teaching about his return and the kingdom of God in this parable?

Was the servant with one talent diligent with it? Why, or why not?

What else can the "talents" represent?

Ask God to reveal "talents" that he has given to you, whether one or ten.

Tell him you want to diligently use all your abilities and strengths for his glory.

Pray for wisdom in using your talents.

What kind of attitude did Paul say slaves should have toward masters? (5)

Who were they really serving? What difference should that make to them?

What should be your attitude at home?

Pray that God will help you "serve wholeheartedly" in whatever you do.

Confess any lack of diligence in responding to your parents, who are like "masters".

Ask God to help you do his will.

What kind of "work" is the writer referring to? Can "love" be a kind of work? (10)

Diligence to do what? Why? (11)

How can one be "lazy" in the Christian life? What is diligent "faith and patience"? (12)

Pray that God will help you be diligent in faith and love, and be strong to the end.

Consider your "hope" of eternal life (heaven) as a reason to be diligent.

Ask God for good models to imitate.

Learning the Way

Our Family Way 13 ~ Concerning WORK in our family

We are diligent to complete a task promptly and thoroughly when asked.

Commentary

Laziness has many faces, including slowness in completing a task, and the failure to complete all of a task. Promptness and thoroughness are barometers of your integrity and your reputation. God wants us to give our whole heart to every task.

Character: Diligence

Working hard on a task and keeping at it until I finish it.

Scripture Memory: Proverbs 13:4

The sluggard craves and gets nothing, but the desires of the diligent are fully satisfied. (NIV)

The soul of the sluggard craves and gets nothing, but the soul of the diligent is made fat. (NASB)

The soul of a sluggard desires, and has nothing; but the soul of the diligent shall be made rich. (NKJV)

Story Starter

"Please set the table for dinner, dear." Kim, curled up on the couch, was irritated that her mother's request came just as she was getting to the best part of her new book. She frowned, ran to the dining room and hurriedly threw forks and napkins onto the table. As she turned to go back to her book, she frowned again, but this time because she knew she had not done her job very well. She went back, put out the glasses and other utensils, and made everything neat and pretty. Just then her mother arrived with a chicken casserole—her favorite! What might have happened if Kim had left her task undone?

Notes _____

_____

_____

_____

_____

_____

_____

_____

Our Family Way

Concerning WORK in our family

14

We take initiative to do all of our own work without needing to be told.

Our Family Way 14

Concerning WORK in our family

Ask A Question

Read The Bible

Day 1

If you earned medals for taking initiative, how many would you have? Why?

Describe the typical day of a child who takes initiative. Do the same for a lazy one. Which one are you usually most like?

Proverbs 6:6-11

Solomon instructs his son about living wisely. He exhorts him to take initiative, and not to be a lazy "sluggard" (a popular figure used throughout Proverbs). He points to the ant.

Day 2

Think of five things you could take initiative to do around the house, without having to be asked or told. Write them down.

Who is someone you know who should be called Mr. or Miss or Mrs. Initiative? Why?

Colossians 3:22-25

Paul instructs slaves of his day how to relate to their masters. His advice to household servants is full of general principles we can use in our own relationships as a family.

Day 3

Look around. How many things can you see that are out of place that you could put away without having to be asked or told?

Read the passage three times out loud, then have each child try to repeat it.

James 1:22-25

James, the brother of Jesus, explains that when we look into the word of God, we must actively choose to do something about what we have seen there, or else we will forget it

---

Day 4

Create a full sentence describing a person with initiative using words beginning with the letters of the word "initiative".

Describe your life if you never took initiative in anything. Would you like it?

Titus 3:12-14

In his closing thoughts to his disciple, Titus, the Apostle Paul exhorts him to take initiative to find and help his friends, and to instruct the people to take initiative in their lives.

Day 5

Think of five specific acts of service toward other believers that you could initiate.

Describe a way you initiated a specific act of ministry or service to another family member. How did you feel about it? How did they?

John 13:12-17

During his final hours with his disciples in the upper room, Jesus took initiative to teach and model the things he wanted them to know before his death. He did not waste any time.

We take initiative to do all of our own work without needing to be told.

Talk About It

Speak To God

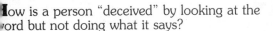

What wisdom do you gain by considering the "ways" of the lowly little ant?

What ways can you be more like the ant in your life at home? with friends?

What is the "sluggard" like? (9)

Pray that God will prompt your spirit to take initiative in all areas of your life.

Confess any spirit of laziness that tempts you to become like the sluggard.

Pray that you will grow in initiative.

What does it mean to "obey" when the master is not looking? Why would you?

What attitude should the servant have about work? What is his motivation?

How can you do the same at home?

Ask God to help you be obedient, especially when your parents aren't watching.

Tell God that you want to be a "wholehearted" child who will please him.

Tell him how you will take initiative today.

How is a person "deceived" by looking at the word but not doing what it says?

How should we "look" into the word? (25)

Why is initiative important when you read the word? What is its relation to blessing?

Express to God your desire to be a doer, not just a forgetful hearer, of his word.

Thank him for his word.

Make a commitment to God to read his word every day, and ask for his help.

What things does Paul ask Titus to do? Will that require some kind of initiative?

What does Paul tell Titus that the Christians in his church must learn to do? (14)

How can one live a "productive" life?

Ask God to show you other Christians to whom you can initiate and minister?

Pray that you will learn to take initiative in caring for your family and friends.

Thank God for his care for your family.

Normally, the servant would wash the guests' feet. Why did Jesus initiate it? (14)

What example did Jesus set for his disciples? How do you think they felt?

How can you imitate Jesus' example?

Praise God that Jesus came to serve us and to save us from our sin.

Ask God to help you learn how to take initiative to serve other people.

Thank Jesus for his example of service.

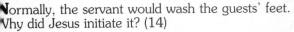

Learning the Way

Our Family Way 14 ~ Concerning WORK in our family

We take initiative to do all of our own work without needing to be told.

Commentary

The most trusted, and rewarded, worker is the one who does not need constant supervision and reminding. He tells himself what to do. The one who will not work unless or until it is necessary or required of him is the sluggard.

Character: Initiative

Doing what needs to be done without needing to be asked.

Scripture Memory: Proverbs 6:6-8

Go to the ant, you sluggard; consider its ways and be wise! It has no commander, no overseer or ruler, yet it stores its provisions in summer and gathers its food at harvest. (NIV)

Go to the ant, O sluggard, observe her ways and be wise, which, having no chief, officer or ruler, prepares her food in the summer and gathers her provision in the harvest. (NASB)

Go to the ant, you sluggard! Consider her ways and be wise, which, having no captain, overseer or ruler, provides her supplies in the summer, and gathers her food in the harvest. (NKJV)

Story Starter

Elizabeth and Ben had a whole Saturday morning to do just as they pleased. Their mom had left for two hours to pick up an out-of-town guest and told them they could play just as soon as they got their chores done. Not long after she had driven away, the two soon became distracted by other more pleasant pursuits. Fortunately, Ben's conscience reminded him that they were playing but they had not done their chores. He found Elizabeth and together they did their work. What would have happened if Ben's conscience had not spoken to him?

Notes

Our Family Way 15

Concerning WORK in our family

We work with a cooperative spirit, freely giving and receiving help.

Our Family Way 15

Concerning WORK in our family

Ask A Question

Read The Bible

Day 1

In general, would you rather be a helper, or be helped, in your family? Why?

Look at each person and identify a specific job or special project for which you would especially want their help.

Ecclesiastes 4:8-12

The Teacher, traditionally considered to be Solomon, compares the emptiness of being alone in life with the wisdom of having a companion in life or work, or for when you fall.

Day 2

Name five activities around the house that you cannot do without cooperating.

Name five more activities around the house that you can do alone, but could just as easily do with someone else's help.

Psalm 133

In this psalm of ascent (for the journey up to Jerusalem for the feasts), the psalmist likens the unity of Israel to the oil of anointing on a priest, and to the snow on a mountain top.

Day 3

If your family were a machine, what part, or function, would each family member be?

Try this: one person is blindfolded and the other's hands are tied behind his back. Now, help each other eat breakfast.

1 Corinthians 12:14-20

Paul uses the human body to illustrate how the body of Christ should function. Each part is important on its own, for its special function, and yet it is dependent on the other parts.

Day 4

Your Bible study accepts families from a smaller group, but the new children don't feel included. What can you do?

What "random acts of cooperation" can you commit in your family today?

Acts 6:1-7

Greek and Hebrew speaking Jews didn't get along well in the new church in Jerusalem. They had to find a way to cooperate and work together for the good of the whole body.

Day 5

Whenever you choose to be cooperative with others, what other attitudes and character qualities must you exercise?

Who is the most cooperative person you know? Describe that person.

1 Thessalonians 2:6b-9

Paul reminds the Thessalonians that he, and other disciples with him, did not come to them to be a burden, but to work with them out of a genuine love and concern for their welfare.

We work with a cooperative spirit, freely giving and receiving help.

Talk About It

Speak To God

Why is the man in verse 8 sad?

What reasons does the Teacher give to say that "two are better than one"? Is that true in your family? Explain?

Who is the third strand of cord in v.12?

Thank God for all the extra "strands" of cord in your life who help you.

Pray that God would let you be a strand in someone else's life in your family.

Thank him for helping you be strong.

Why is it "good and pleasant" for brothers (and sisters) to "live together in unity"?

How does the psalmist describe unity? (2)

Describe what it is like when you live with, and without, unity at home.

Praise God for the Holy Spirit who unifies Christians, and Christian families.

Ask God to help you become more cooperative with your siblings.

Thank him for the blessings of unity.

What is the point Paul is making about unity by using the body as an illustration?

What would happen if you had to function without a hand or an eye?

How is your family like the body of Christ?

Thank God for the unique contribution each member makes in your family.

Pray that he would help you be dependable, and learn to depend on others more.

Tell him how you need each other.

What was the church's problem? What was the solution? Would it be easy?

How did the people cooperate to solve the problem? (note Greek names, v.5)

What was the result of the solution? (7)

Pray that God would help you see new ways to cooperate more at home.

Ask for his guidance in finding solutions to family problems together.

Thank him for the Helper, his Spirit.

What was the attitude of Paul and the others who ministered in Thessalonica?

What did they do so they would not become a burden? What was their attitude?

How was Paul like your parents?

Thank God for your parents who work together to help you know God's truth.

Ask God to help you cooperate with your parents as they obey him.

Pray that you will make their job easy.

65

Learning the Way

Our Family Way 15 ~ Concerning WORK in our family

We work with a cooperative spirit, freely giving and receiving help.

Commentary

The body of Christ is characterized by unity, mutual ministry, and fellowship. In the same way, it is God's Spirit at work when family members look for ways to help others without expectation of recognition or reward, but just for the blessing of it.

Character: Cooperation

Joyfully working with others to do more in less time than I can do by myself.

Scripture Memory: Ecclesiastes 4:9-10

Two are better than one, because they have a good return for their work: If one falls down, his friend can help him up. But pity the man who falls and has no one to help him up! (NIV)

Two are better than one because they have a good return for their labor. For if either of them falls, the one will lift up his companion. But woe to the one who falls when there is not another to lift him up. (NASB)

Two are better than one, because they have a good reward for their labor. For if they fall, one will lift up his companion. But woe to him who is alone when he falls, for he has no one to help him up. (NKJV)

Story Starter

Joy and Jackson loved the falling leaves of autumn. At least until dad handed them each a rake. "Make a pile big enough to jump in," he said with a wink, "and then we'll get some hot chocolate." At first, they just raked everywhere. Then Joy suggested they rake next to each other. The wide trails made it seem like they were getting more done, and they raked to the rhythm of some of their favorite songs that they sang together. It was so much fun, they were sorry it was already done. How did cooperating affect their work?

Notes _____

_____
_____
_____
_____
_____
_____
_____
_____

Our Family Way 16

Concerning WORK in our family

We take personal responsibility to keep our home neat and clean at all times.

Our Family Way 16

Concerning WORK in our family

A → Ask A Question

R ↓ Read The Bible

Day 1

If you owned your own business, how would you deal with lazy workers?

If you earned one penny for being diligent, and lost one for being lazy, would you have earned or lost pennies yesterday?

Proverbs 12:24

In Proverbs, one of the most common contrasts is drawn between the responsible and the irresponsible person—such as one who works hard versus one who is lazy.

Day 2

What could you do to help your family if suddenly you lost everything you had and your father was no longer able to work?

Name at least five good reasons that could motivate you to do your chores.

Proverbs 31:10-31

The portrait of the "noble wife" that closes the book of Proverbs reveals a woman who takes responsibility for every area of her life, and her family's life. She is an exemplar of industry.

Day 3

Imagine that you no longer have to be responsible for anything or anyone. Would you be happier? Why, or why not?

Name all of the things, tasks, and people for which you must be responsible.

Proverbs 12:11, 18:9

Many proverbs express principles that will help people live wise and prosperous lives. The contrast is often between what will happen if you do them, and if you do not do them.

Day 4

Imagine that you are poor and need help. How would you want Christians to treat you, think about you, and help you?

Imagine that you are very wealthy. What would you do to help the poor?

Acts 4:32-37

Luke summarizes what was happening in the new church in Jerusalem, emphasizing their generosity, and the responsibility the growing body of believers felt for meeting needs.

Day 5

Talk about the big and small burdens each family member carries. Identify them and describe what they look like.

If you were backpacking, how much of your tired friend's stuff would you carry?

Galatians 6:2-5

As Paul concludes his letter defending his doctrine of justification by faith alone, he tells the Galatians that it is in caring for one another that the law of God is truly fulfilled.

We take personal responsibility to keep our home neat and clean at all times.

Talk About It

Speak To God

What is "diligence"? What is "laziness"?

Why will the diligent person "rule"? Who will he rule over? How will he rule?

Why would laziness cause one to become "slave labor"? What does that mean?

Pray that God would help you to become more diligent in your daily work.

Confess any laziness in your life.

Ask God to help you understand what it means to be responsible.

Name some of the things that the noble wife does? Could you do all of them?

What are the "affairs of her household"? What is the "bread of idleness"? (27)

What motivates her to work so hard?

Ask God to show you all the things for which your parents must be responsible in order to provide a good home for you.

Thank God that you have a good model of responsibility to follow.

What kinds of "fantasies" might you chase that would keep you from working?

Why is irresponsibility (being "slack") in work compared with "one who destroys"?

What is the "land" you must work?

Ask God for discernment (judgment) in the use of your time and energy.

Tell God that you want to be wise and prosperous, not a fantasy-chaser.

Pray for ways that you can be responsible.

What does it mean that they were "one in heart and mind" and "shared everything"?

For whom did the church accept responsibility? What did they do?

Can we be like them today? Why or why not?

Praise God for his Spirit who unifies your family in love and purpose.

Pray for opportunities for your family to responsibly help the poor and needy.

Pray to become like the early church.

What is the "law of Christ"? (*love*) Why does it fulfill that law when you "carry each other's burdens"? Would anything else?

What attitudes must you have? (3-4)

Whose burdens are you bearing?

Praise God for the law of the love of Christ that works within your spirit.

Ask God to show you burdens in your family's lives that you can share.

Pray for a servant's heart for others.

Learning the Way

Our Family Way 16 ~ Concerning WORK in our family

We take personal responsibility to keep our home neat and clean at all times.

Commentary

A house may be owned by the parents, but the home within its walls should be "owned" by each person who lives there, uses it, and enjoys it. It is simple courtesy, even love, that should drive every family member to help keep it neat and clean.

Character: Responsibility

Choosing to do what I know I should do because it is the right thing to do.

Scripture Memory: Proverbs 12:24

Diligent hands will rule, but laziness ends in slave labor. (NIV)

The hand of the diligent will rule, but the slack hand will be put to forced labor. (NASB)

The hand of the diligent will rule, but the slothful will be put to forced labor. (NKJV)

Story Starter

No one liked housecleaning, but everybody liked a clean house. One day, mother gathered all the children in the den and said, "I hereby officially deputize each of you for the fight against grime in our home. I expect you to help me arrest the mess!" She swore them in as deputies, pinned a badge on each child, and assigned "territories" for each one to guard. Like a good deputy, each child took initiative after that to police their part of the house, and to help others, too. Is that what taking personal responsibility means?

Notes

Our Family Way 17

Concerning ATTITUDES in our family

We choose to be joyful, even when we feel like complaining.

Our Family Way 17
Concerning ATTITUDES in our family

Ask A Question

Read The Bible

Day 1

Think of ten things that really bug you. If they all happened to you today, how could you "rejoice in the Lord always" anyway?

If you knew Jesus would return soon, how would that change your attitudes?

Philippians 4:4-7

In his letter to the Philippians, a church that brought him great joy, Paul exhorts them to overcome their little differences, and even their worries, by living in the joy of the Lord.

Day 2

How much "fruit of joy" grew on you during this past week? What could you make out of it (juice, snack, feast, etc.)?

Re-name as many fruits as you can using "joy" in the name (ex., "joyrange').

Galatians 5:22-26

Paul defends his doctrine of salvation by faith alone and freedom in Christ. We live by the power of the Holy Spirit, not the Law, which is evidenced by the fruit of the Spirit in our lives.

Day 3

You're a finalist in the "Most Joyful Child" competition. You have to reach 10 on the joy meter. What will you do to win?

What goal have you persevered to accomplish that gave you great joy to complete?

James 1:2-4

James, the brother of Jesus, writes to instruct believers how to live wisely and well. Since they are being persecuted, he shows that even trials can bring joy, and lead to maturity.

Day 4

As a family, make up a new song of rejoicing using all or part of Psalm 100.

What are your family's secrets of a joyful life that you can pass down to your children? Write them down together.

Psalm 100

A well-known psalm sung by the Jews to give thanks to God for his love and faithfulness. Thankfulness comes from a worshipful heart that is full of praise and the joy of the Lord.

Day 5

If there was a law that said you had to be joyful always, what would you do?

If you could buy joy, how much would you be willing to spend? Would you buy a little, just enough, or a lot? Why?

John 15:9-14

Jesus, in the upper room on the night before his crucifixion, encourages his disciples. He reminds them that his and the Father's love for them is to be their main reason for joy in life.

We choose to be joyful, even when we feel like complaining.

Talk About It

Speak To God

ow do you "rejoice in the Lord"?

hat do "gentleness" and the "the Lord is near" ave to do with rejoicing?

hen is it okay to "be anxious"? How do you ain "peace" and how does it relate to joy?

Rejoice in the Lord! He is near! Tell him why he makes your heart joyful.

Confess any worries that have replaced the Lord's joy and peace in your heart.

Rejoice that Christ is coming soon.

here is only one "fruit," but it has several quali-es. Picture and describe each one.

ince there is no "law" that requires you to be yful, why should you be?

ow can you "live by the Spirit"?

Confess any sins that would prevent the Holy Spirit's fruit growing in your life.

Ask God to fill your heart and life with the fruit of his Spirit—love, joy, peace.

Pray that you will "live by the Spirit."

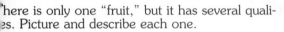

 there any "trial" that would not apply to James' ll to "consider it pure joy"?

hat is the reason you can find joy even in a ial? What is "perseverance"? (3)

hy is "maturity" a reason for joy?

Thank the Lord for any trials that you are fac-ing, regardless of what they are.

Ask God to help you persevere.

Pray that God would work in your life to help you become mature and complete.

entify all the words in this psalm that express he joy of the Lord" in some way.

hat reasons does the psalmist give for that joy d thankfulness? (3,5)

hen does God want us to be joyful?

Thank the Lord that he is God, that he has made you, and that you belong to him.

Praise him for his goodness, love and faithful-ness to every generation.

Rejoice in the Lord! Rejoice!

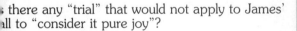

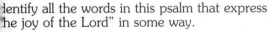

ow can obeying Christ's commands have any-ing to do with love and joy?

hat did Jesus mean by "my joy"? (11)

hat was Christ's "command"? How could that ake their joy complete? (1)

Tell Jesus that you want to obey his commands, and know his love and joy.

Pray that he will show you how to love others in the same way that he loves you.

Ask God to give you a joyful heart.

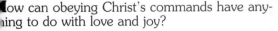

Learning the Way

Our Family Way 17 ~ Concerning ATTITUDES in our family

We choose to be joyful, even when we feel like complaining.

Commentary

We may not always feel "happy" about a situation or a decision, but we can always choose to have a joyful spirit and attitude. When we complain, we are self-centered. When we seek joy, we are choosing to draw on the power of the Holy Spirit.

Character: Joyfulness

Happiness in my heart that comes out on my face and through my words.

Scripture Memory: Philippians 4:4-5

Rejoice in the Lord always. I will say it again: Rejoice! Let your gentleness be evident to all. The Lord is near. (NIV)

Rejoice in the Lord always; again I will say, rejoice! Let your gentle spirit be known to all men. The Lord is near. (NASB)

Rejoice in the Lord always. Again I will say, rejoice! Let your gentleness be known to all men. The Lord is at hand. (NKJV)

Story Starter

Emily had planned for this summertime picnic all week long. Her good friend, Tasha, had come over the day before to help bake cookies, and then spent the night with her. They got up early to make the sandwiches and put everything in the basket. Just then they heard a big roll of thunder. "Girls," said Emily's mom, "I'm so sorry, but it's raining." Emily started to feel sad, but Tasha smiled hopefully. "Come on, Emily," she said, "we can still have our picnic." How were the girls able to be happy despite the disappointment?

Notes

_____

_____

_____

_____

_____

_____

_____

_____

Our Family Way 18

Concerning ATTITUDES in our family

We choose to be peacemakers, even when we feel like arguing.

Our Family Way 18

Concerning ATTITUDES in our family

A Ask A Question

R Read The Bible

Day 1

If your words were seeds, describe what is growing from yesterday's sowing.

Create an acronym or acrostic using the letters of the word "wisdom" to describe the wisdom that God gives.

James 3:13-18

James instructs his readers that God's wisdom is freely available to all. The wisdom of this world brings only disorder, but the pure wisdom from heaven brings peace.

Day 2

Create your own "be-happy-attitudes." Think of at least eight "beatitudes" that would help to promote peace in your home. (ex., Blessed are the joyful...)

Which is better: when others make you feel good, or when you make others feel good? Why?

Matthew 5:1-12

In the Sermon on the Mount, Jesus explains why loving others from a new heart is more important to God than mere lawkeeping. He starts with the blessings of "beatitudes."

Day 3

Have a contest. See who can go the longest today without complaining or arguing. Winner gets a special prize. Discuss it.

What situations push your "argue and complain" button the fastest?

Philippians 2:14-18

Paul writes to one of his favorite churches to thank them for their generosity. He reminds them that God has prepared them to be a shining example of love and unity in Christ.

Day 4

See how many real or real-sounding words you can make using the word "peace". (ex., peacemaker, peacekeeper, etc.)

When do you feel closest as a family? When do you feel separated? Why?

Ephesians 4:1-6, 31-32

Starting in chapter 4, Paul instructs the Ephesians in how to "walk in the light" as believers. One of the first things he mentions is the need for unity and peace in Christ.

Day 5

Come up with your family's Top Ten List of "Dumb Things We Quarrel About."

If God gave you the special gift of being able to end quarrels and make peace, what would you do with your gift?

2 Timothy 2:22-26

In his final pastoral letter, Paul prepares Timothy to take up the responsibility of leadership. He especially warns him about relationships within the body of Christ.

*W*e choose to be peacemakers, even when we feel like arguing.

 **Talk About It**

 **Speak To God**

Describe the world's wisdom. Describe God's wisdom. What is the difference?

Who, or what, is a "peacemaker"?

How do you "sow in peace"? What will your "harvest of righteousness" look like? (18)

Pray that God would help you, by his wisdom, become a peacemaker.

Confess any ways that you might have sown discord instead of peace.

Thank God for the peace of his Spirit.

The word "blessed" means "happy is." According to Jesus, who is the one who is really happy?

Why are "peacemakers" happy? What is the reason for that happiness?

What is your "reward in heaven"?

Pray through each beatitude, applying it to your own life and attitudes.

Pray especially that you would learn to be a peacemaker with others.

Thank God for his spiritual blessings.

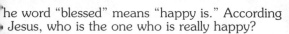

How can you prove to others that you are "children of God without fault"?

What does "do everything" really mean?

Can you "hold out the word of life" if you complain and argue? Why not?

Confess any ways that you complain about things and argue with others.

Pray that God will use you to "hold out the word of life" to your friends.

Thank God that you have his word.

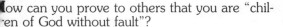

What is the "calling you have received"? What kind of life is "worthy" of a Christian? (1)

What should we "make every effort" to do? What is the "bond of peace"? (3)

What destroys or creates that peace?

Thank God that he has called you to himself and has made you his child.

Pray for a humble, peaceable spirit.

Tell God that you want to become a more forgiving person, like Jesus.

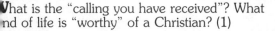

What are some examples of "foolish and stupid arguments" in the church today?

What is the "Lord's servant" like? (24)

How should a mature Christian respond to someone who wants to argue?

Tell God that you want to pursue a life of "righteousness, faith, love and peace."

Confess any argumentativeness.

Pray that God will use you to lead others to him through your gentle spirit.

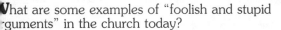

Learning the Way

We choose to be peacemakers, even when we feel like arguing.

Commentary

All families have arguments. Peacemaking, though, means choosing to do whatever is necessary to end an argument rather than win it. It means giving up the right to be right. Jesus said that peacemakers will be "blessed," or happy.

Character: Peacemaker

Finding a way to avoid or end a disagreement rather than to begin or win it.

Scripture Memory: James 3:17-18

But the wisdom that comes from heaven is first of all pure; then peace-loving, considerate, submissive, full of mercy and good fruit, impartial and sincere. Peacemakers who sow in peace raise a harvest of righteousness. those who make peace. (NIV)

But the wisdom from above is first pure, then peaceable, gentle, reasonable, full of mercy and good fruits, unwavering, without hypocrisy. And the seed whose fruit is righteousness is sown in peace by those who make peace. (NASB)

But the wisdom that is from above is first pure, then peaceable, gentle, willing to yield, full of mercy and good fruits, without partiality and without hypocrisy. Now the fruit of righteousness is sown in peace by those who make peace. (NKJV)

Story Starter

Stephan loved having his very own CD player. He had saved his money, and his dad helped him pick out a good one. Now he could listen to his CDs whenever he wanted. He took the player out of the box and set it up in his room. He was listening to his favorite group when Maria, his little sister, came in holding a CD. It was Happy Bear's Church Picnic Songs. Since Maria was too little to have her own CD player, Stephan knew she wanted to use his now. What could Stephan do, and what do you think he did?

Notes _____

_____

_____

_____

_____

_____

_____

_____

Our Family Way 19

Concerning ATTITUDES in our family

We choose to be patient, even when we feel like getting our own way.

Our Family Way 19

Concerning ATTITUDES in our family

Ask A Question

Read The Bible

Day 1

Name the three things that test your patience the most? Why do they do that?

Would you rather build a brick wall, or tear down a brick wall? Why? Which requires more patience? Why?

Proverbs 16:32

Hebrew poetry often uses either contrast or comparison to express an idea. Here Solomon uses both to point out the advantage a man of patience has over a man of strength.

Day 2

Create eight sentences that describe a patient person. Start each sentence with a letter from the word "patience."

What is there about you that others in your family must be patient about?

1 Corinthians 13:4-7

Paul turns to poetry in his letter to the troubled Corinthian church to emphasize the priority of love. He describes what love is, and what it is not. It is the highest of all the virtues.

Day 3

If you were poor, what things would you worry about that you do not worry about now? What about if you were rich?

If you knew the secret to personal peace, who would you tell? Why?

Philippians 4:6-7

Paul tells one of his favorite churches that the secret to knowing and experiencing God's peace is in how we think about and respond to the things that cause us to worry and fret.

Day 4

What is something for which you've had to wait for a long time? While waiting were you patient or impatient? Why?

Have you ever lost something you couldn't replace? What did you pray?

Lamentations 3:19-27

Jeremiah laments about the judgment of God on Jerusalem, yet he knows that God is merciful, too. He knows, though, that he must wait patiently with hope to see that mercy.

Day 5

Do you ever want to be older? Why do you think God made us to have to "grow up" instead of being born an adult?

Do you think you have the patience to be a good farmer? Why, or why not?

James 5:7-11

James encourages Christians who are suffering under oppressors. Jesus will return to judge wrongdoing, but we must wait patiently for that time, and always believe in God's mercy.

We choose to be patient, even when we feel like getting our own way.

Talk About It

Speak To God

Describe the two people being contrasted in this proverb. What are they like?

Why is it better to be a "patient man" than it is to be a "warrior"? Who is stronger?

Which is easier to do? Why?

Ask God to give you a patient spirit.

Confess any ways that you tend to be more like a "warrior" without patience.

Talk to God about the things that might tempt you to become impatient.

What does "love is patient" mean?

Why do you think "love is patient" is the first quality of love in Paul's description?

How does patience affect each of the other qualities mentioned after it?

Pray that God will show you when you are being impatient with others.

Ask him for his grace to be able to love others by being patient with them.

Thank God for his patient love for you.

Identify some family worries or anxieties that this verse would apply to.

What does prayer change? How?

What is the real source of God's peace in our lives? (see also Gal. 5:22)

Tell God the things in your life that tempt you to worry or be anxious.

Thank him that he is faithful and true.

Trust God with your worries so the Spirit can release his peace in your heart.

In spite of great suffering, how did Jeremiah find "hope" in the midst of it?

What is God like to Jeremiah? (25)

What is the response of Jeremiah? What does it mean to "hope"? "wait"? "seek"?

Praise God for his love, compassion, mercy, faithfulness and goodness.

Pray that he will teach you how to "wait quietly" on him during trials in your life.

Tell him your hope is in him.

Why is the farmer and his crop a meaningful illustration of patience? (7)

What effect should the Lord's promised return have on our lives. Why? (8, 9)

Why does James say "don't grumble"?

Pray that you, like the farmer, would be patient, even when wronged by others.

Praise God that Jesus will come again.

Pray that God would help you be patient with others rather than grumble.

Learning the Way

Our Family Way 19 ~ Concerning ATTITUDES in our family

We choose to be patient,
even when we feel like getting our own way.

Commentary

The essence of sin is self-centeredness. Impatience, at its simplest, is selfishness and self-centeredness. It is saying, in words or in attitude, "I don't like this. Change it now!" Getting our own way is getting the wrong way. Waiting patiently is God's Way.

Character: Patience

Keeping a calm spirit while waiting for God to work out his will.

Scripture Memory: Proverbs 16:32

Better a patient man than a warrior, a man who controls his temper than one who takes a city. (NIV)

He who is slow to anger is better than the mighty, and he who rules his spirit, than he who captures a city. (NASB)

He who is slow to anger is better than the mighty, and he who rules his spirit than he who takes a city. (NKJV)

Story Starter

"Anne, I need you to watch the baby while I run to the store to pick up a prescription." Anne looked up at her mom and frowned. "But Mom, the girls outside just asked me to play." Anne's mom sighed. "I understand, but I really need your help right now." Anne watched as her mother juggled her purse and the baby. She went over and took the sniffling baby from her so she could find her keys. As she looked out the door at her friends having fun, and then back at her mom, she made a decision. What do you think Anne decided?

Notes _____

Our Family Way 20

Concerning ATTITUDES in our family

We choose to be gracious, even when we don't feel like it.

Our Family Way 20

Concerning ATTITUDES in our family

Ask A Question

Read The Bible

Day 1

If an angel came to your home disguised as a stranger in need, how would he be treated?

Do you think you've ever met an angel? What happened to make you think so? If not, how do you think you would know an angel?

Hebrews 13:1-3

In reminding his readers to practice hospitality as a normal part of the Christian life, the writer of Hebrews alludes to when Abraham entertained angels. Also read Genesis 18:1-8f.

Day 2

Think of several funny ways you can divide all people into one of two groups.

Identify groups of needy people in your community that you could minister to as a family. (ex., elderly, homeless, latch key kids, etc.)

Matthew 25:31-46

Two days before his crucifixion, Jesus sits with his disciples on the Mount of Olives and tells them the signs to watch for when the end of the age is near, and who God will call.

Day 3

If you could start a church in your home, what would it be like? What would you do for worship? for outreach? for fun?

Think of at least five ministries that you could do in or through your home.

Acts 2:42-47

After Jesus ascended to heaven and sent the Holy Spirit, the new church began to grow. New believers met and ministered in their homes, and helped meet the needs of all.

Day 4

Think of all the ways your family has practiced hospitality in the last year. Who has been ministered to in your home?

If you had an extra room just for guests, what would you do to make it special?

2 Kings 4:8-17

Elisha was a prophet in the northern kingdom of Israel after it split. His ministry was characterized by many miracles, stories of supernatural interventions, and people helped.

Day 5

If you were a traveling evangelist, staying in other people's homes, what kind of hospitality would most encourage you?

If the Apostle John came to stay in your home, what all would you do for him?

3 John 5-8

John's messengers (the "brothers") have been turned away by a church leader. John writes to Gaius, his friend, to thank him for his love and ministry to the messengers.

We choose to be gracious, even when we don't feel like it.

Talk About It

Speak To God

What does it mean to "keep on loving each other as brothers"? How do we?

What does it mean to "entertain strangers"? What is "hospitality"?

How should you treat prisoners? Why?

Thank God for the angels that are watching over you and protecting you.

Pray for opportunities to show humble hospitality to others through your home.

Pray that you'll love other Christians.

Who are the "sheep"? (34,37) Who are the goats"? (41) What are their rewards?

What will Jesus commend the sheep for doing? Why do the sheep question him?

Will Jesus commend you? Why?

Ask God to open your eyes to those around you with needs that you can meet.

Pray for opportunities to minister help and hospitality to others in your home.

Thank God for his love and mercy.

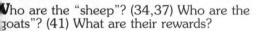

What activities and priorities characterized the new church? Where would they meet?

How did they help needy Christians?

What was happening in the homes of new believers? (46b-47)

Thank God for the body of Christ, your church, and the fellowship you enjoy.

Pray for opportunities to encourage other believers through your home.

Tell God your home is his to use.

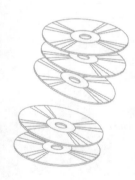

What did the Shunammite woman do to show hospitality to Elisha, a prophet?

How did the woman respond when Elisha offered to speak up for her?

What did Elisha do for her instead?

Thank the Lord for godly people who come into your life to bless you.

Pray for opportunities to minister to missionaries in your home.

Pray for a humble heart to serve others.

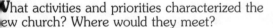
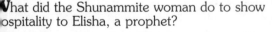
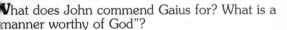

What does John commend Gaius for? What is a manner worthy of God"?

What did John mean that "we ought...to show hospitality to such men"?

Who are such "strangers" in your life?

Thank God for those called to ministry who give their lives to building the body.

Pray for opportunities to minister to visiting ministers in your home.

Pray for God to use your home.

Learning the Way

Our Family Way 20 ~ Concerning ATTITUDES in our family

We choose to be gracious, even when we don't feel like it.

Commentary

God's grace toward us is an act of unmerited favor. We don't deserve it. Our graciousness toward others is an expression of grace. It means treating others the way God would, even when you don't think they deserve it. It is godly courtesy.

Character: Graciousness

Treating all people with the respect they deserve because they are made in God's image.

Scripture Memory: Hebrews 13:1-2

Keep on loving each other as brothers. Do not forget to entertain strangers, for by so doing some people have entertained angels without knowing it. (NIV)

Let love of the brethren continue. Do not neglect to show hospitality to strangers, for by this some have entertained angels without knowing it. (NASB)

Let brotherly love continue. Do not forget to entertain strangers, for by so doing some have unwittingly entertained angels. (NKJV)

Story Starter

Peter squirmed a little in his chair. His mom had asked him to stop by and look in on Mrs. Andersen, an elderly widow down the street. She was alone now since her husband died last year. At first, Peter wasn't sure what to say and he felt uncomfortable. But he thought for a moment and asked, "What was it like when you were growing up, Mrs. Andersen?" The kindly old woman beamed and began to describe her life as a young girl. They had a wonderful visit, and Peter was glad he went. What choice did Peter make to make it a good time?

Notes

_____

_____

_____

_____

_____

_____

_____

_____

Our Family Way 21

Concerning CHOICES in our family

We do what we know is right, regardless what others do or say.

Our Family Way 21

Concerning CHOICES in our family

A → **Ask A Question**

R **Read The Bible**

Day 1

If you could always see God's footprints beside you, how would that affect where you walked, and with whom? Why?

If you could be a tree, what kind of tree would you want to be? Why?

Psalm 1

At the core of the book of Psalms is the belief that God and his truth is at the center of all of life. That central truth is underscored as the theme for all the psalms from this very first psalm.

Day 2

Describe a time when you had to resist others who were trying to entice you to do wrong? What were your thoughts?

Describe the progress and appearance of a sunrise, from dark before the dawn, to full light of day.

Proverbs 4:10-19

In the first nine chapters of Proverbs, Solomon admonishes his son to keep the way of righteousness, as he has done, and warns him to avoid the way of the wicked.

Day 3

Describe a time when you set an example for choosing to do what is right, and how that influenced others to do right.

What special abilities has God given to you that you can use to serve others?

1 Timothy 4:11-16

In his first letter to Timothy, Paul instructs and counsels his younger protégé, both in the practical aspects of the Christian life and in the issues of pastoral ministry in the church.

Day 4

If salvation was a muscle, how would you "work it out" to keep it strong? What would cause it to become weak?

What would cause you to tremble with fear (something real, not imaginary)?

Philippians 2:12-13

Paul encourages the Philippians, based on the example of Christ's sacrifice, to live out their Christianity through obedience, and to yield their lives to God who is working in them.

Day 5

How do you keep a vegetable garden healthy and growing? What must be added or removed in a garden to keep it strong?

What attitude weeds and bugs in your mind need to be killed to keep it strong.

Colossians 3:5-11

As he does in his other letters, Paul exhorts his readers to live out their Christianity in a way consistent with their new identity in Christ...to "become what you are in Christ."

We do what we know is right, regardless what others do or say.

T Talk About It

S Speak To God

What characterizes the "blessed" man? What all does he do and not do?

What is the progress of his actions? (1)

How is the "way" of the righteous man contrasted with the "way" of the wicked?

Pray that God will help you to stay on the "way of righteousness" to be blessed.

Thank God for his word that guides you and for his watching over your way.

Use Psalm 1 as an outline for prayer.

What is one like who stays on the "way of wisdom"? (11) What is one like who walks in the "way of the wicked"? (19)

Where does each "way" lead you?

How bright is the path you are on?

Thank God for your parents who walk on and lead you in the way of wisdom.

Pray that God would help you always turn away from the way of the wicked.

Praise God for his goodness and light.

What kind of example was Timothy to set in speech? life? love? faith? purity?

How was he to minister to others?

How could he "persevere" in "life and doctrine"? How would that save others?

Pray that God would use your faithfulness to him, even as a young person.

Ask that he would show you your own "gifts" and how to use them for him.

Pray for diligence in "life and doctrine."

What verses does the "therefore" refer to? (5-11) Summarize it with a sentence.

What is being "worked out" and "worked in"? Who does each kind of work?

Do you ever have "fear and trembling"?

Praise the Lord for his life, death and resurrection that has saved you.

Pray that God will help you "work out" your salvation to do his will.

Yield your life to God's purpose for you.

What qualities of our "earthly nature" need to be "put to death"? Why? How?

What are some of the sins of the tongue? How do they harm others?

How do you "put on" the new self?

Confess to God any "earthly" sin habits in your life that you need to get rid of.

Thank him for making you a new person with a new heart willing to serve him.

Pray that God will make you more like Christ.

Learning the Way

Our Family Way 21 ~ Concerning CHOICES in our family

We do what we know is right, regardless what others do or say.

Commentary

Integrity and faithfulness to God is more rewarding than popularity and acceptance. The favor of other sinners is fickle and fleeting. It is not worth the risk of displeasing God trying to please others. Doing what we know is right pleases God.

Character: Integrity

Knowing what is right and living that way.

Scripture Memory: Psalm 1:1-2

Blessed is the man who does not walk in the counsel of the wicked or stand in the way of sinners or sit in the seat of mockers, But his delight is in the law of the LORD, and on his law he meditates day and night. (NIV)

How blessed is the man who does not walk in the counsel of the wicked, nor stand in the path of sinners, nor sit in the seat of scoffers! But his delight is in the law of the LORD, and in His law he meditates day and night. (NASB)

Blessed is the man who walks not in the counsel of the ungodly, nor stands in the path of sinners, nor sits in the seat of the scornful; but his delight is in the law of the LORD, and in His law he meditates day and night. (NKJV)

Story Starter

"Hey, Jamie, you've just gotta see this new computer game!" Cody slipped the disk into the CD tray of Jamie's computer as he leaned forward with anticipation. But on the monitor were dark images, evil-looking characters, and disturbing music. He didn't want to offend his friend, or look like a sissy, but Jamie knew this was not the kind of game he should play. He knew Cody might try to talk him into it, so he got up and said, "Thanks, Cody, but I don't think this is a very good game to play." Did Jamie do the right thing?

Notes

_____

_____

_____

_____

_____

_____

_____

Our Family Way 22

Concerning CHOICES in our family

We ask before we act
when we do not know what is right to do.

Our Family Way 22

Concerning CHOICES in our family

A — Ask A Question

R — Read The Bible

Day 1

Which is easier for you: to say "yes" to a wrong thing, or to say "no" to a right thing? Which is worse? Why?

If you could be remembered for doing one good thing, what would it be?

Titus 2:11-14

Paul instructs his trusted disciple, Titus, to help him lead the church, and to know how to face opposition. He reminds him that God's grace provides all he needs to lead.

Day 2

Take this test: 1) Do not think of a blue horse; 2) Think about a lovely sunset. Is there anything you can learn from this test?

In what way, or ways, are you an example that others could follow or imitate?

Philippians 4:8-9

In his closing comments to the Philippians, Paul admonishes them to train their minds to think on things that are "excellent or praiseworthy," and to follow his example.

Day 3

If you knew for sure a priceless treasure was hidden somewhere in the city park, what would you do to try to find it?

There are several paths to choose from. How do you decide which is right?

Proverbs 2:1-11

Solomon, in the first nine chapters of the book of Proverbs, exhorts his sons to follow the way of wisdom, to avoid the way of the wicked, and to diligently seek wisdom wholeheartedly.

Day 4

Starting with "A" and going through the alphabet, come up with 26 words to describe the Bible. (ex., "A is for awesome")

Think of any topic, then identify wisdom from the Bible that can be applied to it.

Psalm 119:97-104

Psalm 119, the longest chapter in the Bible, uses the Hebrew alphabet to teach the worthiness and importance of God's word for living a wise, righteous and godly life.

Day 5

What kind of judge would you prefer—one who judges your actions, or one who judges your attitudes? Why?

If the Bible is really "alive," how do you see it living in your life? Be specific.

Hebrews 4:12-13

The writer of Hebrews, having taught a time of "rest" for God's people is coming, reminds them that, until then, God's word is the standard that will judge their obedience.

---

*W*e ask before we act
when we do not know what is right to do.

T Talk About It

S Speak To God

What does God's grace do in your life? Is it a good "teacher"? Are you a good learner?

What kind of character does God's grace create in you? Why did Christ die for you? Are you "eager to do...good"? How?

Thank God for his grace that teaches you how to be a good and godly Christian.

Express to God that you are willing and "eager to do what is good."

Praise him for our hope in Jesus.

What are some good examples of the kinds of things Paul says to think about?

What is there in Paul's life that you can "put into practice," or imitate?

Are you a good example to others?

Praise God for all the good qualities in this passage that are part of his image.

Ask God to help you practice self-control in choosing what to think about.

Thank him for the apostle Paul's example.

Describe each of the actions Solomon recommends to his son. (1-4)

If he does them, what will his son find? What will God do in his life? (5)

What will be the end result in his life? (9-11)

Praise God for his wisdom and protection that guides you into godly choices.

Tell him that you want to seek his wisdom, diligently with all your heart.

Pray for wisdom and understanding.

What words describe the Bible?

Who is the psalmist like because of his knowledge of the word? (98-100)

How does he think about the Bible? How do you think about the Bible?

Thank God for his word that keeps you on the path of righteousness.

Tell God how much his word means to you, and how important it is in your life.

Pray that you would love his word.

How can the word of God be "living and active"? How is it like a "sword"?

What kinds of "thoughts and attitudes of the heart" does God's word judge? How?

What must we "account" for to God?

Thank God for his word that works deep inside your heart to keep you godly.

Ask God to lead you to scriptures that will help you grow and become mature.

Pray for an open heart for his word.

Learning the Way

Our Family Way 22 ~ Concerning CHOICES in our family

We ask before we act when we do not know what is right to do.

Commentary

There are always many rationalizations for doing something we're not sure is right. Caution and restraint in such a situation are not weaknesses, but qualities of inner strength. The one who is not afraid to ask is stronger than the one who won't ask.

Character: Discernment

Learning to recognize right and wrong so I can choose what is right.

Scripture Memory: Titus 2:11-12

For the grace of God that brings salvation has appeared to all men. It teaches us to say "No" to ungodliness and worldly passions, and to live self-controlled, upright and godly lives in this present age... (NIV)

For the grace of God has appeared, bringing salvation to all men, instructing us to deny ungodliness and worldly desires and to live sensibly, righteously and godly in the present age... (NASB)

For the grace of God that brings salvation has appeared to all men, teaching us that, denying ungodliness and worldly lusts, we should live soberly, righteously, and godly in the present age... (NKJV)

Story Starter

"Hop on, Ben, and I'll take you for a ride." Ben was visiting his cousin, Jake, at their place out in the country. It seemed like there was always something new and different to do whenever his family went there. The thrill of riding on an ATV was really enticing, but something made Ben hesitate before he got on with Jake. He wasn't sure what his parents would think about it, and besides, he noticed there were no helmets. He told Jake, "I'd better check with my parents first." Was Ben being too cautious, or being wise?

Notes

_____

_____

_____

_____

_____

_____

_____

_____

Our Family Way 23

Concerning CHOICES in our family

We exercise self-control at all times and in every kind of situation.

Our Family Way 23

Concerning CHOICES in our family

Ask A Question

Read The Bible

Day 1

Describe a time when you had to be self-controlled. What happened?

Have a self-control contest. Time how long you can keep a straight face while others tell jokes, make faces, and act silly.

Proverbs 29:11

The most repeated contrast in Proverbs is between the way of the wise man the way of the fool—the admonition to choose God-centered wisdom over self-centered folly.

Day 2

You choose the event, and then imagine you are an Olympic athlete. How would you train yourself so you could win?

What are some things you really have to "make yourself" do?

1 Corinthians 9:24-27

Some Corinthians questioned Paul's claim to be a true apostle, like the twelve. He defends himself by comparing his life with an Olympic athlete who must be disciplined to win.

Day 3

Imagine that a wild, ferocious lion is loose in your neighborhood, but you don't know where he is. What would you do?

Describe a time when you were frightened, but you controlled your feelings.

1 Peter 1:13-16 (also 5:8-9)

Peter is writing to Christians who are scattered throughout the Roman world to encourage and strengthen them in their faith in the face of opposition, persecution, and suffering.

Day 4

What would it be like to live in a house with broken windows, and doors that can't be closed? How would you feel?

When are you most vulnerable and in danger of losing your self-control? Why?

Proverbs 25:28 (also 25:26, 27)

The writers of Proverbs expressed their thoughts poetically, often using two related statements, called parallelism. Comparison and contrast are forms of Hebrew poetry.

Day 5

If your heart was a garden and scriptures were seeds, what have you planted there and how is it growing? Which have deep root?

Are you more likely to listen and then speak, or speak and then listen? Why?

James 1:19-21

James, the brother of Jesus, was a writer and teacher of wisdom just like Solomon in the OT. James' wisdom, though just as thoughtful, was more often instructional than poetic.

96

*W*e exercise self-control at all times and in every kind of situation.

Talk About It

Speak To God

Describe someone who gives "full vent" to his anger. Can you reason with him?

What does it mean to keep yourself "under control"? Consider Prov. 29:9.

Why is it foolish to "vent" your anger?

Ask God to help you be self-controlled, no matter what you are feeling.

Pray that you would be wise, and not let your anger control you.

Confess any anger or lack of control.

How is the Christian life like an athletic contest? How do you "win" the contest?

What did Paul mean that he "beat" his body to make it my slave"? (27)

Are you running to win? How? Why?

Thank God for the example of the Apostle Paul's life that you can follow.

Tell God that you want to run in such a way as to win in the Christian life.

Pray that you will be self-disciplined.

What does Peter exhort his readers to do? Identify verbs as attitudes or actions.

What are "evil desires"? What then, in contrast, does it mean to "be holy"?

Is "self-control" a part of being holy?

Pray that God will help you to be mentally prepared and self-controlled in life.

Praise God for his holiness.

Confess any ways that you still desire things that are wrong, or not holy.

What is a "city whose walls are broken down" like? What is its problem?

Why is lack of "self-control" like that city?

Consider Prov. 25:26. How is it similar to 25:28? What is it to "give way"?

Pray that self-control will be like a strong wall of protection around your heart.

Ask God to strengthen your ability to exercise self-control at all times.

Thank him for his Holy Spirit in you.

What character qualities are required to obey the admonitions of verse 19?

Why would "anger" keep a man, or woman, from living a "righteous life"? (20)

What does God's word do? How?

Thank God for his word, planted in your heart, that leads you to righteousness.

Pray that you would be "quick to listen, slow to speak and slow to anger."

Ask God to help you be self-controlled.

Learning the Way

Our Family Way 23 ~ Concerning CHOICES in our family

We exercise self-control at all times and in every kind of situation.

Commentary

Self-control, which is a fruit of the Holy Spirit, is the key to other character qualities. The ability to rule over one's emotions and body is necessary for godliness, and removes the possibility that, in some situation, some one else will have to do it for you.

Character: Self-Control

Choosing to control my thoughts and feelings so they do not control me.

Scripture Memory: Proverbs 29:11

A fool gives full vent to his anger, but a wise man keeps himself under control. (NIV)

A fool always loses his temper, but a wise man holds it back. (NASB)

A fool vents all his feelings, but a wise man holds them back. (NKJV)

Story Starter

Whenever First Church had a potluck dinner, it was a big event. The dinner was first, with all kinds of delicious offerings. The desserts were always put out during the music and lesson time. When the lesson was over, all the kids knew where to go. Ryan studied the spread of desserts and picked one or two he thought he would like best. He noticed his friend Whitney taking much more than she could ever eat. He thought to himself that he would like to try everything, too, but he didn't. Would it have been wrong for Ryan to fill his plate high with dessert?

Notes

_____
_____
_____
_____
_____
_____
_____

We always tell the truth and do not practice deceitfulness of any kind.

Our Family Way 24
Concerning CHOICES in our family

 **Ask A Question**

 **Read The Bible**

Day 1

If your lifespan was shortened by one day for every lie you told, what would you do? How long would you have to live?

If God knows it whenever you lie, why do you lie? Why don't you fear God? Why should you?

Psalm 34:11-16

The psalmist, traditionally identified as David, praises God for his protection of the righteous, and then instructs hearers how to fear God and live a righteous life of "many good days."

Day 2

Have you ever had someone accuse you of something you didn't do? How did you feel? How did you respond?

Could you get a fair trial if witnesses were not required to tell the truth? Why not?

Exodus 20:16, 23:1-2

The ninth commandment emphasizes the priority of honesty in dealing with others. The rest of the law given at Mt. Sinai includes restrictions about even being deceptive.

Day 3

What are seven things that you really don't like? Why don't you like them?

Using different parts of the body, describe the actions of an honest, godly person. (ex., hands that help the poor, feet that…, etc.)

Proverbs 6:16-19

Numerous writers of proverbs, whether Solomon or others of that day, used lists to express their thoughts. The number "seven" often suggested completeness.

Day 4

How have you grown in Christ this year? What have you stopped, or started, doing because you want to be more like Christ?

Is there any difference between a "little" lie and a "big" lie? Why, or why not?

Ephesians 4:20-25

Paul exhorts the Ephesian readers in how to walk in Christ's light. He tells them to stop their "old" sinful habits, and put on Christ, since they have been "made new" in him.

Day 5

How can you tell when someone is not being truthful, or can you? Explain.

What are apparently "playful" ways we can practice untruthfulness or deceit. (false promises, exaggeration, etc.) Should we?

Proverbs 12:19, 22, 15:4

There are many references in Proverbs to honesty and truthfulness in contrast to lying and deceitfulness. Honesty is a basic principle of righteous living and the way of wisdom.

We always tell the truth and do not practice deceitfulness of any kind.

 **T**
Talk About It

 **S**
Speak To God

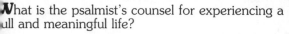

What is the psalmist's counsel for experiencing a full and meaningful life?

Is this all there is to learning the "fear of the Lord"? Why should we fear him?

How do we fear God this way at home?

Praise God that he will, in his time, punish all evildoers in the world.

Tell him you want to "do good" and to "seek peace" in all you say or do.

Ask him to teach you how to fear him.

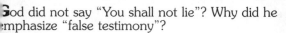

God did not say "You shall not lie"? Why did he emphasize "false testimony"?

Who is protected in each of these laws?

How can you give "false testimony" at home? (sibling arguments, discipline)

Pray that God would help you keep the ninth commandment in your family.

Pray that he would keep you from hurting others with untruthfulness.

Thank God that he is always true.

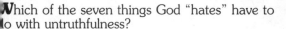

Which of the seven things God "hates" have to do with untruthfulness?

What different parts of the body does the proverb mention? Why?

Where do lies begin? (in the heart)

Praise God that he is a righteous and holy God who hates sin.

Ask God to give you a heart that hates the sins he hates, and loves good.

Pray for a sensitive conscience.

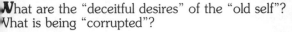

What are the "deceitful desires" of the "old self"? What is being "corrupted"?

How does "the truth that is in Jesus" change us? What is the "new self"? (24)

How, then, should we live? Why?

Confess any sins of deceitfulness that are remnants of your "old self."

Tell God you want to be like him in everything you think, say, and do.

Commit your heart to being truthful.

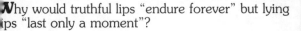

Why would truthful lips "endure forever" but lying lips "last only a moment"?

Why does God "delight" in truthfulness?

What is "deceit"? Can you tell the truth in a deceitful way? How?

Tell God that you want all of your words to be honest and truthful, without deceit.

Confess any ways that you have been even a little bit deceitful or dishonest.

Thank God that he honors truthfulness.

Learning the Way

Our Family Way 24 ~ Concerning CHOICES in our family

We always tell the truth and do not practice deceitfulness of any kind.

Commentary

Dishonesty is a sinful act that, if left unconfessed and then repeated, can lead to a spirit of deceitfulness. We can even learn how to tell the "truth" in a deceitful way. Deceitfulness can become a sinful habit of thinking and speaking.

Character: Honesty

Telling what I know is true without any hint of deception or falsehood.

Scripture Memory: Psalm 34:12-13

Whoever of you loves life and desires to see many good days, keep your tongue from evil and your lips from speaking lies. (NIV)

Who is the man who desires life and loves length of days that he may see good? Keep your tongue from evil and your lips from speaking deceit. (NASB)

A Who is the man who desires life, and loves many days, that he may see good? Keep you tongue from evil, and your lips from speaking guile. (NKJV)

Story Starter

"We could just tell them the cat knocked it off the table," Jordan said as he nervously surveyed the damage with his sister, Wendy. They had been playing in the living room when an errant pillow sent Mother's precious china figurine crashing to the hardwood floor. They knew it would be wrong to lie, but they also knew they would be disciplined for throwing pillows if they told the truth. When their parents returned from their walk, the children had to decide what to do. What do you think the children told their parents?

Notes

_____

_____

_____

_____

_____

_____

_____

_____

We're on the Way!

Our Family Commitment

Trust in the Lord with all your heart and lean not on your own understanding;
in all your ways acknowledge him, and he will make your paths straight.
Proverbs 3:5-6

Train a child in the way he should go, and when he is old he will not turn from it.
Proverbs 22:6

We, the _____ family, having studied and learned these 24 Ways, and the Word of God, now commit together to walk God's path of life as a family. We will "trust in the Lord" with all our hearts, and "acknowledge" him in all of our ways. As parents and children, we will wholeheartedly help each other follow the straight path of life God sets before us, and will not turn from it.

On this date: _____ We're on the Way!

_____   _____

_____   _____

_____   _____

_____

Ways to Be: Related Character Qualities

Way 1: Godliness
Wanting more than anything else to please God in everything that I think, say and do.

Way 2: Trust in God
Remembering every day that God loves me and will take care of me.

Way 3: Reverence
Honoring God, my parents and all proper authorities because of who they are in God's eyes.

Way 4: Submissive
Willingly accepting and following the authorities God has placed over my life.

Way 5: Love
Wanting only the best for others and showing it in how I treat them and speak to them.

Way 6: Service
Doing for others without expecting them to do anything for me in return.

Way 7: Encouragement
Speaking words to others that build them up and lift them up in the Lord.

Way 8: Forgiveness
Treating someone who has offended me as though I had never been hurt.

Way 9: Thankfulness
Being glad and grateful for my life, and showing it.

Way 10: Contentment
Deciding to be happy with my circumstances, whatever they may be.

Way 11: Generosity
Happily sharing with others all that God has given to me.

Way 12: Stewardship
Using wisely everything that God has given to me—my time, my talents and my treasures.

Way 13: Diligence
Working hard on a task and keeping at it until I finish it.

Way 14 Initiative
Doing what needs to be done without needing to be asked.

Way 15: Cooperation
Joyfully working with others to do more in less time than I can do by myself.

Way 16: Responsibility
Choosing to do what I know I should do because it is the right thing to do.

Way 17: Joyfulness
Happiness in my heart that comes out on my face and through my words.

Way 18: Peacemaker
Finding a way to avoid or end a disagreement rather than to begin or win it.

Way 19: Patience
Keeping a calm spirit while waiting for God to work out his will.

Way 20: Graciousness
Treating all people with the respect they deserve because they are made in God's image.

Way 21: Integrity
Knowing what is right and living that way.

Way 22: Discernment
Learning to recognize right and wrong so I can choose what is right.

Way 23: Self-Control
Choosing to control my thoughts and feelings so they do not control me.

Way 24: Honesty
Telling what I know is true without any hint of deception or falsehood.

Ways to Remember: 24 Ways Practice List

Use for prompts for reciting the Ways, or with the practice page in the Kids Color-Book.

Concerning AUTHORITIES in our family...

1   We **love** and **obey** our Lord, Jesus Christ, with **wholehearted** devotion.

2   We **read** the Bible and **pray** to God every day with an **open** heart.

3   We **honor** and **obey** our parents in the Lord with a **respectful** attitude.

4   We listen to **correction** and accept **discipline** with a **submissive** spirit.

Concerning RELATIONSHIPS in our family...

5   We **love** one another, treating others with **kindness**, **gentleness** and respect.

6   We **serve** one another, **humbly** thinking of the **needs** of others first.

7   We **encourage** one another, using only words that **build up** and **bless** others.

8   We **forgive** one another, covering an offense with **love** when **wronged** or hurt.

Concerning POSSESSIONS in our family...

9   We are **thankful** to God for what we have, whether it is **a little** or **a lot**.

10   We are **content** with what we have, not **coveting** what others have.

11   We are **generous** with what we have, **sharing** freely with others.

12   We **take care** of what we have, using it **wisely** and **responsibly**.

Concerning WORK in our family...

13   We are **diligent** to complete a task **promptly** and **thoroughly** when asked.

14   We **take initiative** to do all of our own work without **needing** to be told.

15   We work with a **cooperative** spirit, freely **giving** and **receiving** help.

16   We take personal **responsibility** to keep our home **neat and clean** at all times.

Concerning ATTITUDES in our family...

17   We choose to be **joyful**, even when we feel like **complaining**.

18   We choose to be **peacemakers**, even when we feel like **arguing**.

19   We choose to be **patient**, even when we feel like **getting our own way**.

20   We choose to be **gracious**, even when we don't **feel like it**.

Concerning CHOICES in our family...

21   We do what we know is **right**, regardless what others **do or say**.

22   We ask **before we act** when we do not know what is **right** to do.

23   We exercise **self-control** at **all** times and in **every** kind of situation.

24   We always **tell the truth** and do not practice **deceitfulness** of any kind.

Ways to Keep: Making Our Own Ways

Way Maker(s): _____ Ages(s): _____

Date: _____ Place: _____

Our Family Way: _____
_____
_____
_____
_____

Way Maker(s): _____ Ages(s): _____

Date: _____ Place: _____

Our Family Way: _____
_____
_____
_____
_____

Way Maker(s): _____ Ages(s): _____

Date: _____ Place: _____

Our Family Way: _____
_____
_____
_____
_____

Way Maker(s): _____ **Ages(s):** _____

Date: _____ **Place:** _____

Our Family Way: _____
_____
_____
_____
_____

Way Maker(s): _____ **Ages(s):** _____

Date: _____ **Place:** _____

Our Family Way: _____
_____
_____
_____
_____

Way Maker(s): _____ **Ages(s):** _____

Date: _____ **Place:** _____

Our Family Way: _____
_____
_____
_____
_____

Other Our 24 Family Way Resources

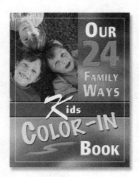

Our 24 Family Ways resources are available from Whole Heart Online (www.WholeHeart.org), and at Christian bookstores everywhere.

Our 24 Family Ways Kids Color-In Book Younger children in your family will be thrilled to have their own coloring book with all the Ways and illustrations, an O24FW practice sheet, and an "I'm On the Way" certificate of excellence that you can date and sign when they can recite all the Ways.

Our 24 Family Ways Laminated Poster Get this colorful 11"x17" laminated poster of the 24 Family Ways to hang on your wall or fridge to help in learning the Ways. (Available only on WHOnline)

Our 24 Family Ways Flip-a-Way Chart This calendar-style table-top flipchart is a fun way to review the Ways. Full Way faces forward; fill-in-the-blank Way faces out. Or, turn it around. Spiral-bound with easle. (Available only on WHOnline)

Free Downloads from WHOnline You can visit our website to download free O24FW resources such as Scripture memory verse card templates, Bible story suggestions for family times, and other helps. They are in the Family Toolbox.

About Whole Heart Ministries

Whole Heart Ministries is a non-profit Christian home and parenting ministry dedicated to encouraging and equipping Christian parents to raise wholehearted children for Christ. Whole Heart Press, our ministry publishing arm, is committed to writing, finding and publishing "books to build hearts for God." Whole Heart Online, our ministry website, is dedicated strengthening your family to serve God wholeheartedly. Go there to find all of our books, events information, recorded messages, articles, parenting resources, free downloads, helpful information, and much more. For more information, visit us online:

www.wholeheart.org

About the Author

Clay Clarkson is a wholehearted father of four wholehearted children. Prior to beginning Whole Heart Ministries with his wife Sally in 1994, Clay served on staff with Campus Crusade for Christ, in overseas missions, and on the pastoral staffs of several churches. He is a graduate of Denver Seminary. He has authored several other books, including **Educating the WholeHearted Child** with WHPress, and **Heartfelt Discipline** and **The Great Dadventure** (2005) with WaterBrook Press. He has edited several reprints of old books and written numerous articles. He loves to teach the Bible to "renew the mind" with God's truth, and is an acoustic guitarist, singer and songwriter.